TRUE HERO

"The true story of the extraordinary mission of God"

Can God be trusted?

Learning to love God's Word

True Hero
Student Discipleship Guide
Published by Wheaton Press © 2020
Wheaton, Illinois

www.WheatonPress.com

ISBN-13: 978-1-950258-15-4
ISBN-10: 1-950258-15-7

1. Christian Education – Discipleship 2. Spiritual Formation – Discipleship. 3. Culture & Theology – Education.
4. Nonfiction-Religion and Spirituality-Christian Life. 5. Nonfiction-Spiritual Growth-Christ-centered.

Contact the publisher for discounted copies for partner schools and receive free resources and training for teachers.

Learn more at WheatonPress.com or email WheatonPress@gmail.com

AGENT NAME:

TRUE HERO

"The true story of the extraordinary mission of God"

WANTED
By Order of the Sanhedrin
PAUL
REWARD

Equipping Students to Reflect
Christ in their circles of influence

	YEAR ONE	YEAR TWO	YEAR THREE
Growth Emphasis	An Emphasis on Belonging	An Emphasis on Identity	An Emphasis on Purpose
Essential Questions	1. How do I understand God's Word? 2. How do I love God's Word?	3. How do I approach God? 4. How do I relate to God, myself and others?	5. How do I make sense of the world? 6. Who will I follow?
Essential Outcomes	Understand and articulate the Christ-centered Narrative	Develop authentic Christ-centered relationships	Develop a clear Christ-centered personal mission
Courses	HiStory, The Mission of God and the secret of the Golden Thread True Hero	The X things God wants you to know about Himself ID: Learning to relate to God, myself and others	TALMIDIM; the path of the disciple Witness & Worldview
Leadership Pipeline	D Groups	Mentor Project	The Glory Project
Answering the Essential Questions	Belonging: Where do I fit?	Identity: Who am I?	Purpose: What will I do?

Essential Questions

1. How do I understand and love God & His Word?
2. Can I trust that Jesus is the Messiah?

Stages in the Investigation

1. Plot
2. Prologue
3. Patriarchs
4. Passover
5. Pillar
6. Promised
7. Proximity

Course Description

Students will examine the reliability of the testimony of one of the most unusual trials in history. Students will be challenged to objectively investigate historical as well as eyewitness accounts of the events and make up their minds regarding the claims that are made.

This is not a survey course but an introduction to the person of Jesus Christ, His life, death, resurrection, and claims to be God in the flesh. Students will be challenged by the testimonies of personal transformation and be invited to embrace a personal relationship with the God of the Bible.

Students will interact with the disciplines of language, literary analysis, archeology, geography, and history while having the opportunity for a personal application and personal contribution. Students will produce several unique and distinct projects to demonstrate understanding and provide opportunities to practice creativity while building relational and communication skills.

Remember your Creator in the days of your youth before the days of trouble come...
Ecclesiastes 12:1

Course Overview

True Hero invites students on an investigative journey to evaluate the trustworthiness of the Bible and the claims that it makes. Throughout the journey, students will examine the plot and four significant motifs within the story of Scripture to investigate the reliability of the claims and how they apply to their lives.

Learning Outcomes

A Students will examine historical texts; applying the principles and skills of critical reading to cite textual evidence to support analysis of what the text says explicitly as well as inferences from the text.

B Students will analyze testimony, claims, and historical statement for accuracy and reliability.

C Students will identify and examine main events and developments within the overall plot of the Bible and be able to sequentially connect characters, geography, and motifs into the whole historical plotline.

D Students will build upon the foundation for understanding the concepts of worldview, and integration as discipleship, by examining the theme of the Kingdom and glory of God that is introduced in Genesis 1 and culminates in Revelation 22.

E Students will be challenged to exercise personal creativity and critical thinking through project-based learning assessments designed to invite the communication of understanding and application.

F Students will demonstrate an understanding of the concepts they have learned by applying them through a cross-disciplinary project that is designed, assembled, developed, and constructed by their class.

Beliefs Values Habits Actions

Course Overview

Unit 1. Plot

1. What is the learning goal for this course?
2. What can I expect from this course?
3. What will my personal contribution be?
4. Can I communicate the plot of the Hebrew Scriptures?
5. What is the rising action that leads to Act 2?
6. What happens in the 400 years of silence?
7. Who are the characters and what is the setting of Act 2?
8. What is close reading and how do I read life a detective?

Unit 2. Prologue

1. Is the eyewitness testimony trustworthy?
2. Who are the eyewitnesses?
3. What do the eyewitnesses say?
4. Does the eyewitness testimony fulfill the prophecies from the Hebrew Scripture?
5. What do I find meaningful about the prophecies that were fulfilled by Jesus of Nazareth?

Unit 3. Patriarchs

1. Who is Jesus of Nazareth?
2. Did Jesus of Nazareth claim to be the Messiah?
3. Is Jesus the Christ?
4. Can we trust that the miracles of Jesus were real?
5. What happened at Cana?
6. Are the miracles of Jesus fact or embellished fiction?
7. Does the life of Christ fulfill the lives of the Old Testament patriarchs?
8. Did Jesus claim to be God?

Unit 4. Passover

1. Did Jesus rise from the dead?
2. What is the connection between the two gardens?
3. Does the resurrection matter?
4. What are alternate theories to the resurrection?
5. What do the witnesses say?
6. What does the evidence say?
7. Can I trust the resurrection is real?

Unit 5. Pillar

1. What happened at Pentecost?
2. What is the role of Acts in the plot of Scripture?
3. What is the connection between Acts 2 and the Old Testament Threads?
4. Did the lives of the followers of Jesus reflect that they believed in the resurrection?
5. Who is Paul and how does he live the mission of the Golden Thread?
6. What was it like to reflect Christ in the ancient world?
7. How will I communicate learning in a creative and meaningful way?

Unit 6. Promised

1. What is the future Kingdom of God?
2. How do we know that we can trust the prophecies regarding the coming Kingdom of God?
3. How is the purple thread fulfilled in Act 2, scene 5?

Unit 7. Proximity

1. What did my investigation reveal?
2. What was the result of Paul's trial?
3. What is my investigation summary?
4. What difference will this make in my life?

TRUE HERO

"The true story of the extraordinary mission of God"

plot

Learning to love God's Word

The Jerusalem Times

Extra! Extra! Extra!

Governor Festus seeks private Investigators to help with Trial!

Dateline: Act 26

King Agrippa and his sister Bernice have arrived in Caesarea to pay their respects to Governor Festus.

They have been spending many days here, and yesterday Governor Festus discussed the ongoing trial of Paul from Tarsus with the King.

According to Festus, "the chief priests and the elders of the Jews brought charges against Paul and asked that he be condemned."

The new Governor did not delay the case, but convened court the next day and ordered Paul to be brought in.

When his accusers got up to speak, they did not charge him with any of the crimes Festus had expected.

Instead, his accusers had some points of dispute with him about their own religion and about a dead man named Jesus who Paul claims is alive.

At a loss about how to investigate the matter, Festus asked if Paul would be willing to go to Jerusalem and stand trial there.

But Paul made an appeal to be held in Caesarea and to stand trial before Caesar in Rome.

Yesterday, Festus was overheard telling King Agrippa that he believed Paul had done nothing deserving of death, but because he had made his appeal to the Emperor, he decided to send Paul to Rome.

The rumor is that because he has nothing definite to write to Caesar about Paul both Festus, and King Agrippa, will conduct further investigations to determine what will be written because they believe "it is unreasonable to send a prisoner on to Rome without specifying the charges against him."

What is the learning goal for True Hero?

The Sanhedrin vs. Paul of Tarsus

Help Wanted!

CLASSIFIED

Immediate openings for qualified candidates.

By order of Governor Festus and King Agrippa, qualified candidates are invited to apply to join an elite investigation team.

The team will be responsible for investigating the accusations against and the oral defense of Paul of Tarsus.

Must be able to

- approach the evidence objectively,
- think critically,
- read like a detective,
- work well with others,
- have a strong understanding of the plot of the Hebrew Scriptures.

Dear Candidate,

Word has reached the ears of Governor Festus and King Agrippa about the museum that your class created and your knowledge of the plot of the Hebrew Scriptures.

As a result, scholars have recommended your class apply to be part of the investigation team.

If you choose to apply and are accepted, then you will be asked to examine the evidence in the case of Paul of Tarsus. Paul is currently facing the possibility of a trial before Caesar.

Aliases of this man include; Saul of Tarsus, Saul the Pharisee, Paul, The Apostle Paul, Paul the Missionary to the Gentiles.

Paul stands accused of many "serious but unproven charges."

Your job will be to investigate the facts of the case and submit your findings and recommendation to Governor Festus and King Agrippa. To qualify as a member of the investigation team, you must pass a basic competency assessment and demonstrate an understanding of the plot of the Hebrew Scriptures.

Qualified Candidates will then be required to attend Detective training to ensure that all members of the team use the same methods during the examination of the evidence and interviews with the key witnesses.

Upon completion of the training, you will conduct your investigation in seven stages.

1.Prologue. Investigate the Jewish Prophecies concerning their Messiah and the claim by Paul that Jesus Christ fulfilled the prophecies.

2. Patriarch. Investigate the life and claims of Jesus of Nazareth. Are the reports that he performed miracles reliable? Did He claim to be God?

3. Passover. Investigate the claim that Jesus rose from the dead? Is the evidence reliable?

4. Pillar. Investigate the lives of the Disciples of Jesus. Travel to Jerusalem, Greece, and Rome to follow in the footsteps of Paul and his associates.

5. Promised. Investigate Paul's claim that Jesus will return to earth in the future.

6. Proximity. Consider the evidence and submit your findings.

7. **Shalom**. An opportunity to reflect.

Investigation Team Qualifying Assessment

Thank you for your interest in serving your King and your country.

Qualified candidates will be joining an elite team of Detectives to investigate the claims of Paul of Tarsus regarding Jesus of Nazareth. A man who Paul claims is not only the Jewish Messiah but that he rose from the dead.

To qualify for the team, you must pass a basic assessment demonstrating your understanding of the plot and characters of the Hebrew Scriptures.

To demonstrate your understanding, you will give an oral overview of the plot of the Old Testament using the seven stages as your outline.

Part I. Create a Timeline

You will create a personal timeline of the Old Testament using the seven stages that were used in the class Museum as your outline. Start by identifying significant events and characters in the plot, but keep the content focused by focusing on the main elements of the plot, as illustrated in the four threads.

Then personalize your timeline with illustrations and pictures. You are encouraged to be as creative as you want. Your timeline should accurately reflect the information while, at the same time, be a reflection of your personality.

Part II. Oral Presentation

Once you have completed your timeline, you will be asked to present the full plot of the Hebrew Scriptures informally to a friend or family member outside of this class. Your presentation can be made in an informal conversational manner using your completed timeline as a visual aide.

Presentation Rubric

Directions: Your student desires to qualify for an elite investigation team into the accusations against Paul of Tarsus regarding his claims about Jesus of Nazareth.

To qualify, they must demonstrate a basic understanding of the plot of the Hebrew Scriptures using the seven key scenes and the four key motifs. The presentation is designed to be informal and can be completed at a dinner table or other casual environment.

Please listen carefully and use the rubric to help aide us in determining whether or not to issue your student an invitation to join the team of elite investigators.

The Bible is

ONE STORY

TOLD IN
TWO ACTS

BOTH ACTS HAVE SEVEN SCENES

1 2 3 4 5 6 7

ACT I BEGINS BY INTRODUCING US TO THE MISSION OF GOD AND ENDS WITH 400 YEARS OF UNREST AND SILENCE.

1 2 3 4 5 6 7

ACT II BEGINS BY INFORMING US THAT GOD IS COMMITTED TO FULFILLING HIS MISSION, AND ENDS WITH ETERNAL SHALOM

THE BLUE THREAD

THE BLUE THREAD

PROLOGUE

PATRIARCH

PASSOVER

PILLAR

PROMISE

PROXIMITY

SILENCE

The Blue Thread

PROLOGUE

John. There came a man sent by God. His name was John. He said the Messiah was coming and called the people to repent.

PATRIARCH

Jesus. Jesus was born. He was the very incarnation of God. He fulfilled God's promises. He obeyed God's will and reflected His glory to the nations through His sinless, life, death and resurrection.

PASSOVER

Cross. Jesus died on a cross for the sins of all people as God's final Passover lamb. He was buried and rose again from the dead after three days. He invites people from all nations to be reconciled with God, reflect His will, and live for His glory.

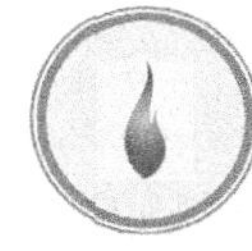

PILLAR

Church. Jesus returned to heaven, and God sent His Spirit to fill His people with His presence. The Holy Spirit empowers people to invite people from all nations to be reconciled with God, reflect His will, and fill the earth with His glory.

PROMISE

Second Coming. Someday Jesus will return from Heaven. Those who have trusted Him to forgive them will be with Him forever.

PROXIMITY

New Earth. There will be a new heaven and a new earth. The glory of God will come from heaven and fill the earth and people from every nation will worship Him forever.

SHALOM

Shalom. God's mission is complete.

Tell the story...

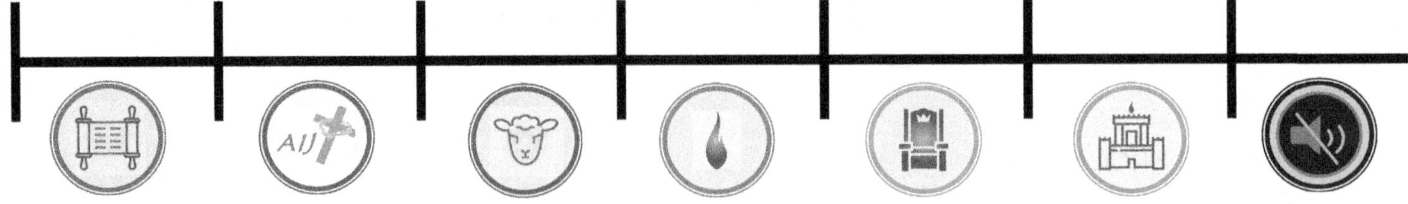

PROLOGUE

PATRIARCH

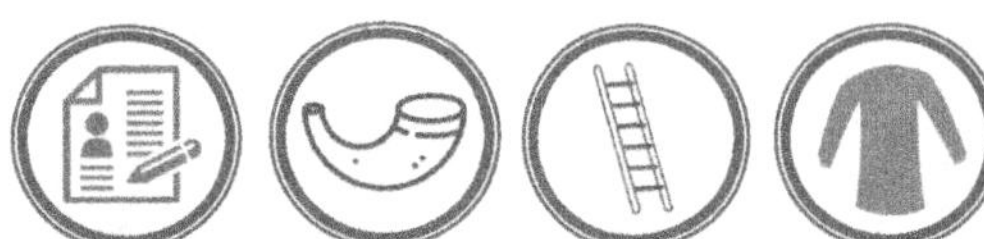

PASSOVER

PILLAR

PROMISE

PROXIMITY

SILENCE

What is the climax of Act I and what is the falling action and the resolution?

Climax. This is often considered the most exciting or suspenseful part of the story. The turning point; the point of greatest suspense or action.

Falling Action. In what way is the action in this part of the story different from the first part? Action and events that occur after the climax.

Resolution. How does this part of the story make you feel? The end of the story is where the conflicts or problems are solved.

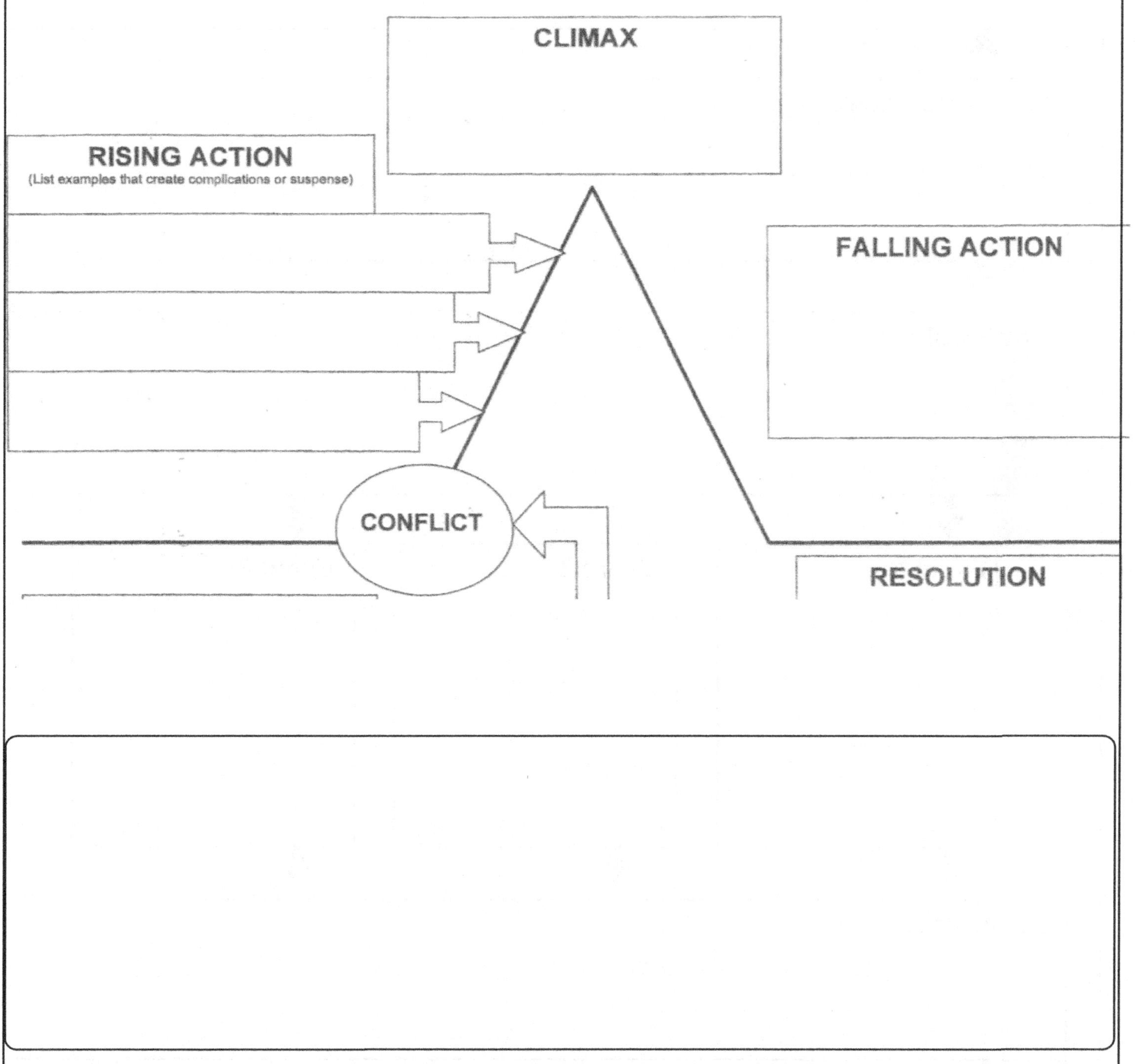

What are the rising action and the conflict that lead up to the beginning of Act 2?

Rising Action. What events occurred leading up to the beginning of Act II?

Conflict. What types of conflict are present in the story?

Setting:
Where:

When:

Major Characters:

Minor Characters:

Plot/Problem:

Event 1:

Event 2:

Event 3:

Outcome:

The 400 years are anything but "silent."

Even though they are commonly called the 400 years of silence, many essential things occur between the end of the Hebrew Scriptures and the beginning of the Gospel accounts of the life of Christ.

In the Hebrew Scriptures, God brings the people of Israel to the land that He promised, and the threads of the Old Testament plot converge at the dedication of the Temple.

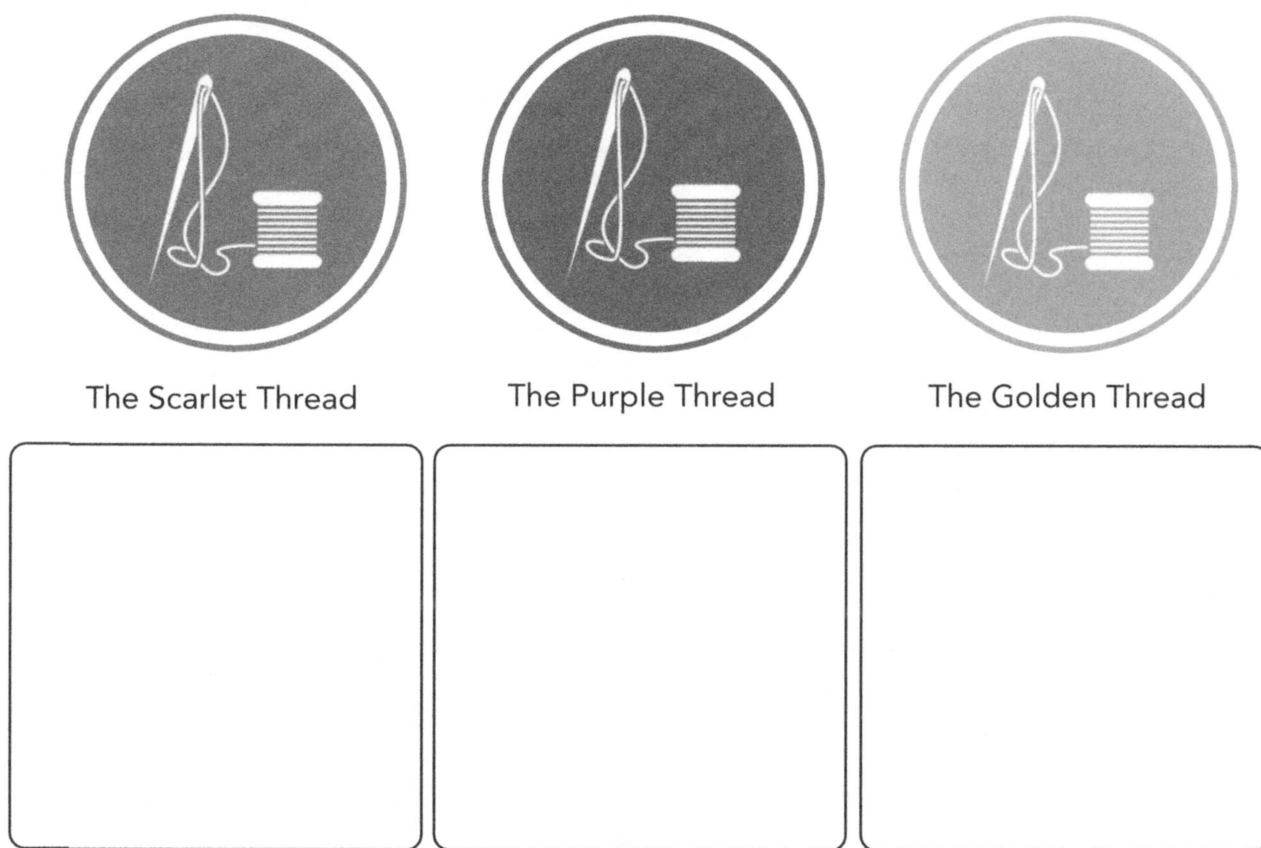

After Babylon destroys Jerusalem and The Temple of God is destroyed, the Jewish culture adapts to their new reality during their exile in Babylon.

There is no temple, and Pharisees, Sadducees, and rabbis replace the role of priests.

A system of synagogues focused on educating the people and calling them back to obedience to the law is added to daily life.

The influence of the Greeks and the Romans through Hellenization and Pax Romana create conflicts and opportunities that lead to some people longing for the promised Messiah and others believing that perhaps God had forgotten His promise to His people.

PURPLE THREAD

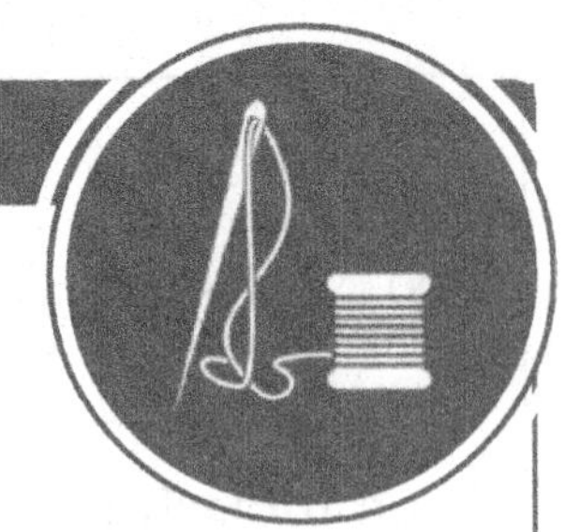

THE KINGDOM OF GOD

God. In the beginning, God created the heavens and the earth.

Eden. God created male and female in His image and entrusted humans with His mission to reflect His will and fill the earth with His glory. Nothing separates them and no shame exists.

Jacob. Jacob was a deceiver. He lied to his father, stole from his brother, and wrestled with God. But God showed grace to Jacob and changed his name to Israel. He became the father of the 12 tribes of Israel.

Moses. Moses was born. He encountered God in a burning bush. God told Moses he would be the deliverer of God's people.

Pillar. When the descendants of Israel left Egypt, The Spirit of God led His people in a cloud by day and a pillar of fire by night.

Sinai. God invited Moses into His presence and gave His people His law. He told them to reflect His glory to the nations. If they obeyed, then He would bless them and if they disobeyed, they would be punished.

Tabernacle. God told His people to make a tabernacle that would reflect His glory to the nations, remind people of the Garden, and be the place where they could be forgiven.

Ark. Inside the Tabernacle was a holy place. God told His people to make an Ark and to place it inside. God filled the tabernacle with His presence.

Temple. Solomon built God a temple. The Temple reflected God's glory to the nations, reminded people of the Garden, and was the place where they could be forgiven. The Ark was placed inside The Holy Place and God filled the temple with His presence.

Jesus. Jesus was born. He was the very incarnation of God. He fulfilled God's promises. He obeyed God's will and reflected His glory to the nations through His sinless, life, death and resurrection.

Church. Jesus returned to heaven and God sent His Spirit to fill His people with His presence. The Holy Spirit empowers people to invite people from all nations to be reconciled with God, reflect His will and fill the earth with His glory.

Second Coming. Someday Jesus will return from Heaven. Those who have trusted Him to forgive them will be with Him forever.

New Earth. There will be a new heaven and a new earth. The glory of God will come from heaven and fill the earth and people from every nation will worship Him forever.

GOLDEN THREAD

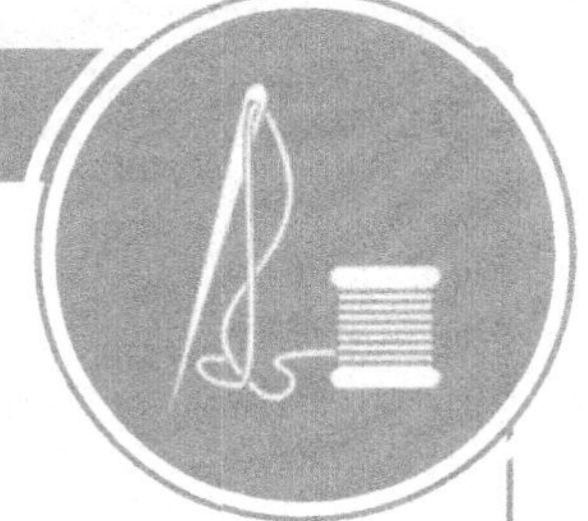

THE MISSION OF GOD

Glory. For the earth will be filled with the knowledge of the glory of the Lord...

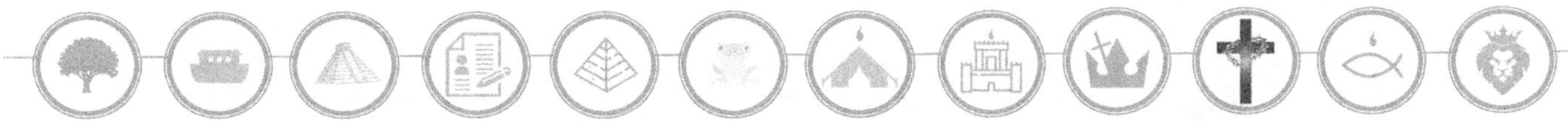

Eden. God created male and female in His image and entrusted humans with His mission to reflect His will and fill the earth with His glory. Nothing separates them and no shame exists.

Noah. The earth filled with evil. God told Noah to build an ark. God demonstrated His perfect justice by flooding the earth to cleanse it and His perfect grace by providing an ark to preserve humanity. God entrusts Noah with His mission to fill the earth with His glory.

Babel. The nations of the world rebel. They start to build a tower to heaven so they would not be scattered. But God confused their language and scattered them over the earth.

Abraham. God gives His mission to Abraham and tells Him to go. Abraham trusted God and obeyed. Abraham had two sons, Ishmael and Isaac.

Egypt. Joseph was Israel's favorite son. His brothers betrayed him, and he became a slave in Egypt. Joseph trusted and obeyed God. God showed favor to Joseph. He became a leader in Egypt. Josephs brothers and their families came to Egypt. They were fruitful and multiplied. 400 years later a new Pharaoh enslaved the descendants of Israel.

Plagues. Moses trusted and obeyed God. But Pharaoh disobeyed God. God sent plagues to show the nations that He is the only God.

Tabernacle. God told His people to make a tabernacle that would reflect His glory to the nations, remind people of the Garden, and be the place where they could be forgiven.

Temple. Solomon built God a temple. The Temple reflected God's glory to the nations, reminded people of the Garden, and was the place where they could be forgiven. The Ark was placed inside The Holy Place and God filled the temple with His presence.

Jesus. Jesus was born. He was the very incarnation of God. He fulfilled God's promises. He obeyed God's will and reflected His glory to the nations through His sinless, life, death and resurrection.

Cross. Jesus died on a cross for the sins of all people as God's final Passover lamb. He was buried and rose again from the dead after three days. He invites people from all nations to be reconciled with God, reflect His will, and live for His glory.

Church. Jesus returned to heaven and God sent His Spirit to fill His people with His presence. The Holy Spirit empowers people to invite people from all nations to be reconciled with God, reflect His will and fill the earth with His glory.

New Earth. There will be a new heaven and a new earth. The glory of God will come from heaven and fill the earth and people from every nation will worship Him forever.

SCARLET THREAD

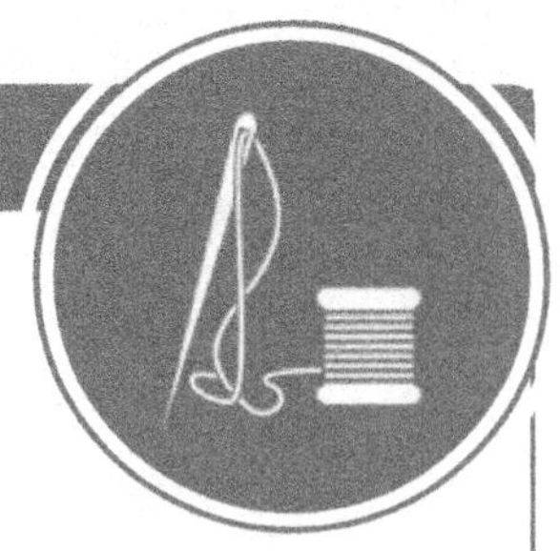

PLOT SUMMARY

Redemption. "Hallelujah! Salvation and glory and power belong to our God,

Adam. Adam and Eve chose to reflect their own will and seek their own glory. Sin causes disintegration. Adam felt fear and hid from God. The consequence of disobedience was death and separation from God. But God substituted the blood of an animal to cover their shame, remove their sin, and reintegrate humanity with Himself and His mission.

Noah. The earth filled with evil. God told Noah to build an ark. God demonstrated His perfect justice by flooding the earth to cleanse it and His perfect grace by providing an ark to preserve humanity. God entrusts Noah with His mission to fill the earth with His glory.

Isaac. God told Abraham to go to offer Isaac as a sacrifice. Abraham trusted God and obeyed. God provided a ram as a substitute. Isaac had two sons, Esau and Jacob.

Passover. God told His people to prepare a special meal with a lamb. God showed grace to those who trusted and obeyed. Pharaoh let God's people go.

Tabernacle. God told His people to make a tabernacle that would reflect His glory to the nations, remind people of the Garden, and be the place where they could be forgiven.

Temple. Solomon built God a temple. The Temple reflected God's glory to the nations, reminded people of the Garden, and was the place where they could be forgiven. The Ark was placed inside The Holy Place and God filled the temple with His presence.

John. There came a man sent by God, His name was John. He said the Messiah was coming and called the people to repent.

Cross. Jesus died on a cross for the sins of all people as God's final Passover lamb. He was buried and rose again from the dead after three days. He invites people from all nations to be reconciled with God, reflect His will, and live for His glory.

Student Timeline Presentation Rubric

To be completed by the individual listening to the presentation

Student Name: ______________________ Listener's Signature: ____________________

Listener's Name: ______________________ Date: ____________ Date: ____________

	1	2	3	4	Total
Organization	Presentation has little to no organization	Presentation is somewhat organized but has sequencing issues that demonstrate lack of practice and distract from understanding.	Presentation follows a logical and well-organized sequence.	Presentation is logical, informative, entertaining and demonstrates both learning and understanding.	
Information	Little to no research is evident. Student does not even cover two -two main points of learning.	Some research is evident, but student does not fully grasp the material or only three - four main points of learning is reflected upon.	Student reflection and research is evident, but only five - six main points of learning are reflected upon.	Student clearly learned, understood and made application to seven main elements of learning through the semester.	
Visual	No visual is presented for this assignment.	The presentation included some visual support, but it was basic in nature and added little to the ability of the audience to clarify or understand.	The presentation included a relevant visual that was not a distraction.	The presentation included a creative visual aide that demonstrated initiative, creativity, engagement while clarifying their presentation in a significant manner.	
Delivery	The student is not prepared to present and/or forgot their paper/presentation/visual .	Student mumbles, incorrectly pronounces material, and/or speaks too quietly to be heard.	The student speaks with a clear voice and they pronounce theological or technical terms with accuracy.	Material is accurately presented in a clear, engaging and meaningful manner.	
Total					

Congratulations!

Welcome to the team!

Your understanding of the Hebrew Scriptures qualifies you to become a member of the investigative team.

As a member of the team, your mission will be to investigate the claims of Paul of Tarsus regarding Jesus of Nazareth. Paul is accused by the Sadducees of claiming that Jesus was not only the Jewish Messiah but that He rose from the dead.

Through the process of your investigation, you will need to read witness statements, examine the evidence, and follow the clues to decide if Paul is telling the truth or if he is worthy of imprisonment.

To accomplish your mission, you will need to

1. Read like a detective.

2. Preserve your evidence. (Cite your source, book, chapter, verse).

Key Words

Detective – Individual who researches and gathers information to solve mysteries.

Clue – A fact or object that helps to provide an answer to the unknown.

Mystery – Something that is secret or unknown.

Evidence – Something that helps uncover or demonstrate truth.

Read like a Detective

A. Good Detectives check all their sources and decide if they are reliable.

Sourcing

Before reading a text ask…

- Who wrote this?
- What is the perspective of the author?
- When was it written?
- Where was it written?
- Is it reliable?
  - Why or Why not?

B. Do the witness statements contradict each other or corroborate with each other?

Corroboration

- Do other documents exist?
- If so, then what do they say?
- Do the documents agree?
- If not, why?
- What document or documents are the most reliable?

Read like a Detective

Contextualization

- **When** and **where** was the document created?
- **What** was different during that time period?
- **What** was the same?
- How might the circumstances in which the document was created affect the content?

C. Good Detectives examine all evidence and decide if it is reliable.

Event Sequence

As you read, notice the order in which things happen or ideas are presented. Think about the beginning, middle and end.

- Events are the important actions that move the plot forward.
- Sequence is the order that the events happen.
- Signal words are clues to help clarify the order of events.

D. Good Detectives notice the sequence of events?

Read like a Detective

E. Good Detectives decide if the witnesses are making statements that are facts or opinions.

Fact vs. Opinion

How do you know something is true? It is important to know the difference between a fact and an opinion.

- **A fact is a statement that can be proved or verified.**
- **Facts are certain and true.**
- **An opinion is a statement of personal belief or feeling.**
- **Opinions vary.**

F. Good Detectives compare and contrast events, perspectives and testimony from various sources.

Compare & Contrast

How are things alike and how are things different?

- To compare means to tell how two or more things are alike.
- To contrast means to tell how two or more things are different.
- Signal words can help you to compare and contrast.

Read like a Detective

Inferences

Authors may hint at an idea without stating it directly. You must use what you already know about a topic to make a connection and figure out what is being communicated.

- You make an inference by combining text clues with your background knowledge to arrive at a logical conclusion or an "educated guess."

Good Detectives examine the evidence and make inferences.

Summarize

Think about how to retell the key idea of a text in your own words. What are the most important details to help you get to the point?

- The topic is the focus of the passage. What is the passage about?
- The important details add more information about the topic.
- A summary is a brief statement of the topic using the most important details.
- A good summary is short and clear.

You will need to summarize events, witness testimony and your conclusions so that King Agrippa and Governor Festus can read your decision.

Read like a Detective

How to write a summary

A summary is a shortened version of a longer reading that tells the basic ideas of the text or passage.

A summary should be

A. Short (3-5 sentences).
B. Focused on the main ideas.
C. Use both your words AND key words from the text.
D. Be focused on the description and not include opinion or personal feelings about the text.

Reading Response

- If this text were a stand-alone story or chapter, then what would be a good title to help explain it?
- What is the main point or big idea of the text?
- Who are the main characters involved?
- What is the setting and how does it impact what does or doesn't happen?
- What is the primary problem, conflict or struggle in the text?
- What are 2 or 3 key events that move the plot?
- Is there a solution that is offered? If so, then what is the solution?

How does Act I connect to Act II?

So many different changes occur between the end of Act I and the beginning of Act II that it is easy to forget that they are two halves of the same story.

In the beginning of Act II, the common language is Greek. The Romans are the ones who occupy the streets of Jerusalem. The visible presence of God over the Temple is gone. The Ark of the covenant is lost. The God-ordained role of the priest has been diminished and there are several new religious and political groups with competing agendas.

Overall, there is a shared desire for the promised Messiah to come and to set up his kingdom on the earth, but disagreement exists as to what needs to be done for that to happen.

The Pharisees believe that righteous living will bring the Messiah, so they have added to the law. The Sadducees oversee the Temple. They are wealthy and powerful, but they reject most of the Hebrew Scriptures and seek power by embracing Greek culture.

Like the Sadducees, the Herodians desired power through politics. In contrast, the Zealots want to rebel against the Romans, and the Essenes are so tired of everyone fighting that they decide to leave Jerusalem and live in caves out in Qumran.

Who are these groups of people? How did all of this happen? How do we fill in the gap between the Hebrew Scriptures in Act I and the Greek Scriptures in Act II so that we can pick up the plot and recognize how the God of the Bible continues the plot into Act II?

Understand the setting and context of the investigation

Five essential elements of a story

Characters. The individuals that the story is about. There should be enough detailed descriptions that the reader can visualize each person. Every story should have a main character.

Setting. The location of the action. The environment or surroundings should be described in detail so that the reader feels that they can picture the scene.

Plot. The actual story upon which the book is based. A plot should have a clear beginning, middle, and end.

Conflict. Every story has a conflict to solve. The plot is centered on this conflict and how the characters attempt to resolve the problem.

Resolution. The solution to the problem. The resolution must fit the rest of the story in tone and creativity, and solve all the parts of the conflict.

Six essential elements of a plot

Exposition. What information does the writer give you at the beginning of the story? How are the setting and the characters established? (conflict, character, setting).

Rising Action. What events in the rising action drew you in the most as a reader? The character attempts to solve the problem but fails.

Conflict. What types of conflict are present in the story? How did you identify them?

Climax. This is often considered the most exciting or suspenseful part of the story. The turning point is the point of greatest suspense or action.

Falling Action. In what way is the action in this part of the story different from the first part? Action and events that occur after the climax.

Resolution. How does this part of the story make you feel? The end of the story is where the conflicts or problems are solved.

What is the setting?

Setting. The location of the action.

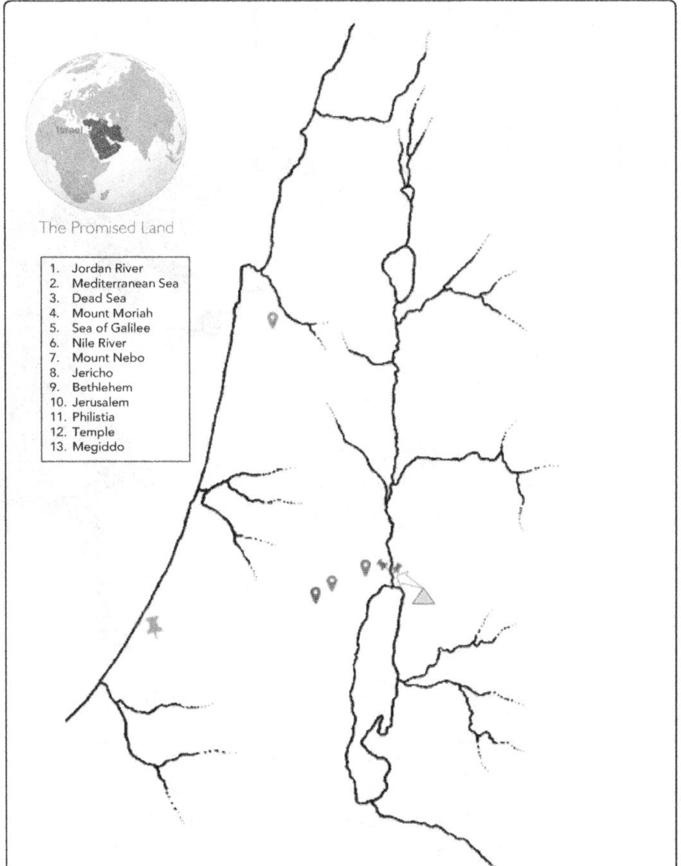

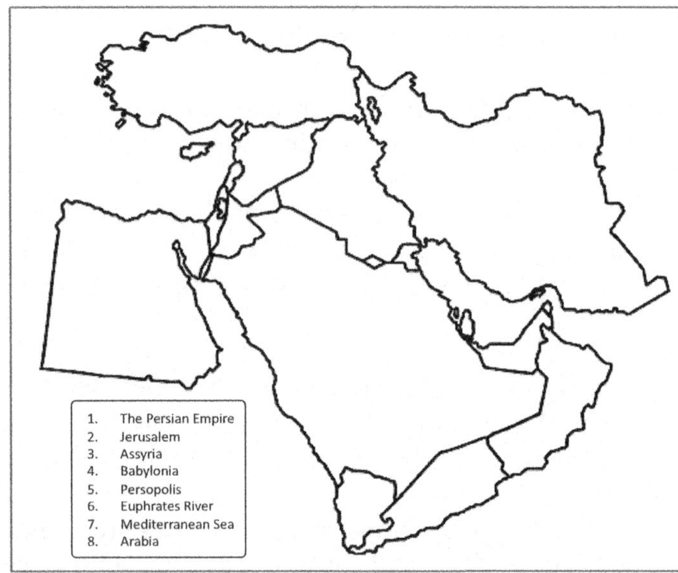

What happens during the last scene of Act I that impacts the start of Act II?

Assyria.

Babylon.

Persia.

Greece.

Rome.

Israel.

The influence & impact of Alexander the Great

Although Alexander the Great is never specifically mentioned by name in the Scriptures, it is impossible to deny the impact that He had on the plot of Scripture and the mission of God.

Alexander's story begins with two thought leaders who have influenced every generation that has come after them. The name of the first one is Plato. The second one is Aristotle.

The "Influencers"

The New Testament illustrates that Greek Philosophers had a massive impact on the way people viewed and understood the world they lived in, leading up to the birth of Jesus Christ. Plato is known as the father of Greek Philosophy.

The Gospel writer, and disciple of Jesus, John begins his testimony about the life of Christ by using a teaching from Plato as the outline for his first chapter. Later John would write the letter known as 1 John as a way to combat some of the negative influence of Plato's teaching on the early church.

Plato had a student whose name was Aristotle. Aristotle was born in the north of Greece in Macedonia. He loved the Greeks and moved to Athens to study under Plato when he was only 17 years old. He learned Greek. He worshipped the Greek gods, and like Plato, he would go on to teach and influence others with his view of the world.

Aristotle had a student who would become a major influencer. His name was Alexander. Alexander was also from Macedonia, and his father asked Aristotle to tutor and mentor Alexander in Greek culture, religion, and philosophy.

After the death of his father, Alexander became the leader of Macedonia.

Understanding the role of Alexander the Great

Undefeated in battle, in just 13 brief years, Alexander conquered most of the known world and introduced a concept known as *Hellenization*.

Hellenization is the idea of making all things Greek through *education*, *language*, and *culture*. It was Alexander's idea not only to conquer the land but to change and influence the culture.

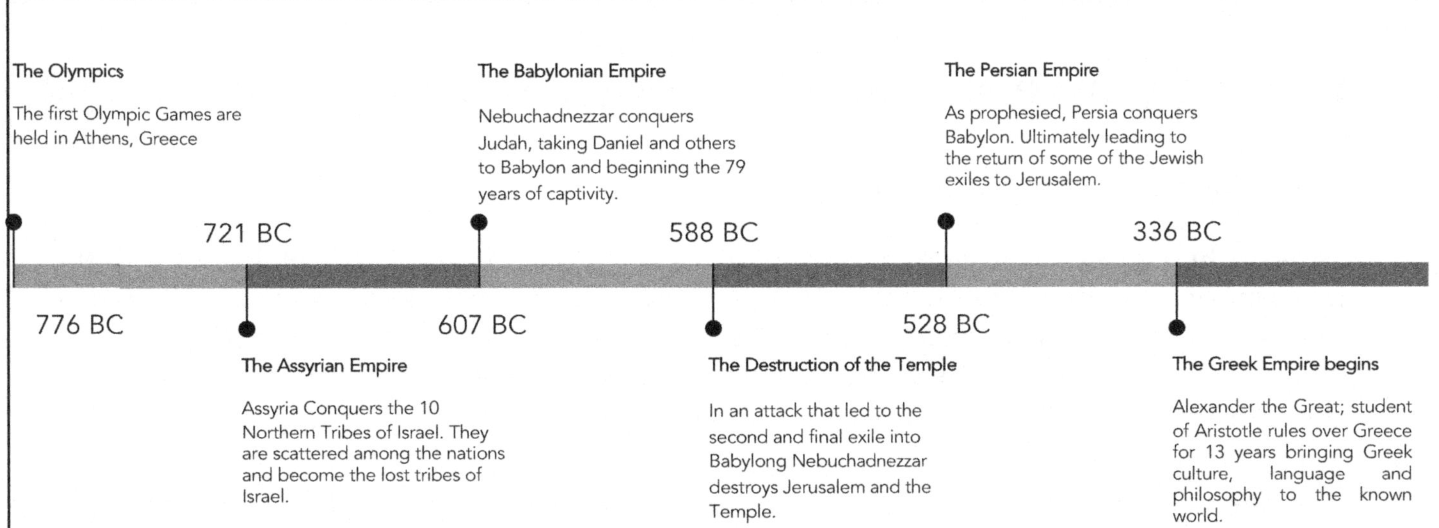

Understanding the influence of Alexander the Great

Hellenism. As Alexander the Great conquered the world through military power, he started schools to teach Greek Philosophy, religion, and Koine Greek to spread the thought and culture of Greece. The word Hellenistic comes from the root word Hellas, which was the ancient Greek word for Greece.

Hellenization is where Alexander had his most influence. Not long after his death, the Roman Empire emerged, and ownership of the land would change hands from Greece to Rome. But Alexanders' influence lived on through the introduction of Greek Philosophy, religion culture, and a common Greek language.

Culture. Jews dispersed throughout the known world as well as those in the land of Israel were influenced by Greek culture in a wide variety of ways. Some were positive as Hellenization, and Pax Romana paved the way for a system of safe roads to connect the known world for Paul and other missionaries.

Learning. Some were more subtle, like the Greek system of education and debate known as the Socratic method. The process of teaching and learning by asking questions is something we see in the interactions between Christ and the religious leaders. As you read through the testimony, watch how many times Jesus responds to a question by asking one in return. This method of teaching was common at the time and emerged under the influence of the Greek Philosopher Socrates.

Later, the Apostle Paul would use the Greek culture of philosophical argument to the advantage of Christianity. Although his missionary journeys took him to many synagogues and other Jewish meeting places, he also addressed Roman citizens in venues specially designed for debate. Acts 17:16-34 speaks of his time in the Areopagus in Athens.

Synagogue. Implemented after the destruction of the Temple during the Babylonian exile, when the people of God no longer had a place where heaven and earth met (purple thread). Even with the building of the second Temple there was no Ark so that mean that the priest could no longer meet with God on behalf of the people (scarlet thread). The result was that the role of the priest was replaced by other religious leaders. The purpose of the synagogue was not to replace the Temple. There were no priests or sacrifices. They were places of education for the purpose of carrying out the Deuteronomic Covenant.

The influence & impact on faith and practice

The influence and the impact

Greek Philosophy. The word philosophy means "*love of wisdom*." Philosophy is the process of organizing thoughts and ideas within a framework or view of the world. Philosophy provides a systemized way of understanding and comparing various worldview perspectives. Alexander the Great's *Hellenization* of the world opened the door for the global influence of Greek Philosophy at the time of Christ.

Polytheism rejects Monotheism. Poly means many. Polytheists, like the Greeks and the Romans, believed in the existence of many gods. In contrast, Monotheists like Jews and Christians who believe that there is one God.

Apologetics. A Greek word meaning "to defend a belief through logical speech and explanation." Greek Apologetical methods influenced the arguments of Peter as well as Paul's defense before Festus and Agrippa (1 Peter 3:15, Acts 26:2).

Language. Alexander's idea was creating a common culture and to infuse the Greek way of thinking and speaking into the known world. One of the results was the spread of Koine Greek. The word Koine simply means common. Koine Greek was different from what is known as **Classical Greek.**

Koine. was spoken by the common people and became a common trade language spoken by Hellenized Jews across Macedonia, Greece, North Africa, and the Middle east. In contrast, classical Greek was limited to the wealthy, educated, upper class.

The Septuagint. As Greek became the common language and some descendants of Abraham lost connection with Hebrew during the Babylonian exile, an effort was made to copy the Hebrew Scriptures into Greek by Jewish Scholars.

The result was a complete copy of the Hebrew Scriptures in Koine Greek called the *Septuagint*. This is the text quoted by most of the New Testament writers, including Christ. For example, it is why the Gospels record the Greek word Christ rather than the Hebrew word Messiah.

The use and understanding of Koine Greek allowed for the Greek New Testament to be copied and carry the message of the Gospel to the world.

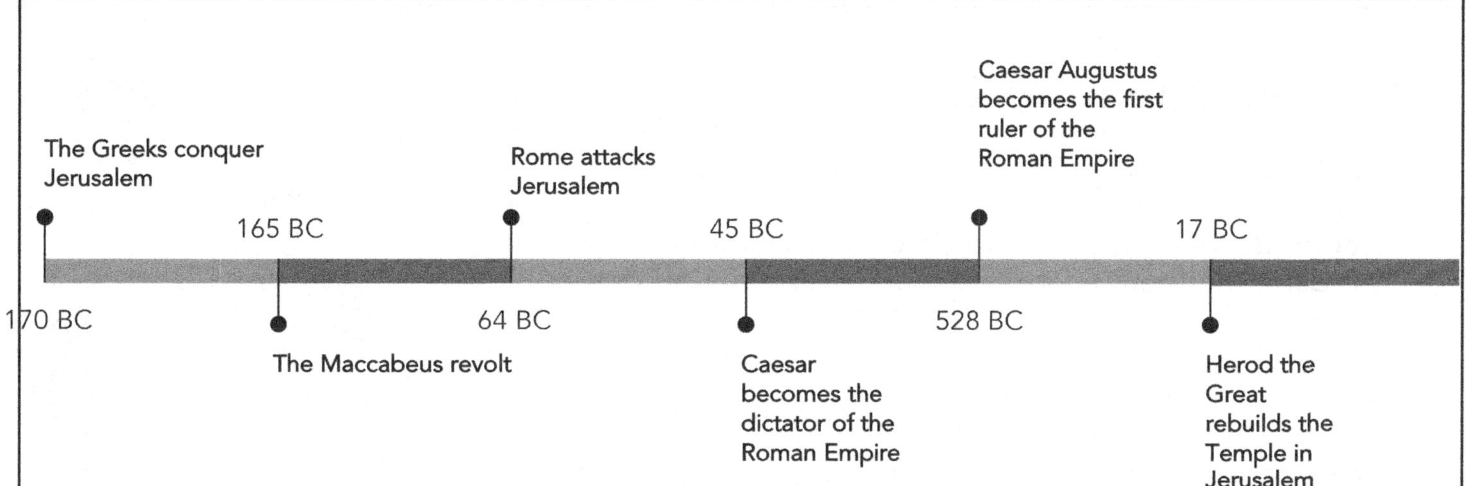

The silent years part II

Here comes the Hammer...

Antiochus III (the Great). The people of God lived in the land but under the control and rule of foreign leaders. As a result, a series of kings and rulers, some good, some not so good, each took a turn ruling over the people of God.

Antiochus the III, known as the Great in an effort not to confuse him with Antiochus the IV who was a tyrant, was one of the good leaders. For their help against his enemies, Antiochus the III, promised to reduce taxes and provide funds for the rebuilding of Jerusalem.

Antiochus IV Epiphanes. Antiochus Epiphanes was a tyrannical Greek king based in Babylon who reigned from 175 BC to 164 BC.

He claimed to be able to **walk on water** and **calm the seas as a god in human form**. Antiochus outlawed the study of Torah and set up an altar in the Jewish Temple where he sacrificed pigs and decreed that all Jews were to eat swine and sacrifice to pagan gods.

Judas Maccabeus. The Maccabeus family led a revolt against Antiochus Epiphanes that led to the restoration and the cleansing of the temple in 165 BC.

Judas declared the Jews were to celebrate the faithfulness of God through an 8-day celebration of lights that would take place in the winter and commemorate the rededication of the Temple of God.

John 10 records Jesus in Jerusalem, celebrating **the Feast of Dedication** that we know today as **Hanukah**.

All roads lead to Rome

Pax Romana & Giving to Caesar what is Caesar's

Rome. Between the last words of Malachi and the first words of Matthew, a lot takes place over a period of 400 years.

The world is a very different place.

The language has changed. The culture has changed. The Jewish people themselves have changed. In many ways, they have forgotten their purpose.

Now, instead of embracing their role as the reflection of God's glory on the earth, they approach their obedience to God's law from the perspective of a transaction.

Deuteronomic Covenant. God's covenant promise to Abraham was unconditional. God would keep His part of the promise no matter what.

But the covenant that God made with the people at Shechem where Joshua read the law out loud to the people, and they promised to give their hearts wholly to God was conditional.

God's desire was to bless Israel for the purpose of His glory that they would be a distinct people out of all the nations of the world. Not for their benefit, but for His glory. Remember that the golden thread of Scripture is the glory of God filling the earth and reaching all the nations of the world.

Israel disobey. They fell into gross sin. Their hearts moved far from God, and He took them out of their land. Now for 400 years, they have lived under occupation, first, from the Greeks, and then from the Romans.

After 400 years, most of the Jewish people had forgotten the purpose of their blessing. They desired that the Messiah, who was promised by the prophets, would come and deliver them from the Romans.

They wanted a Hero! They wanted a modern-day Judge or a brave warrior like David to remove the giant of Rome from their midst so they could enjoy the benefits and blessing of God again.

In the minds of the Jewish people, the Romans were the giant that was keeping them from that blessing. The good news was that the exile had ended their idolatrous ways, and God had miraculously and supernaturally preserved His people and their culture. But the bad news was that they forgot their purpose and they were expecting the wrong Messiah.

Understanding the tension in Jewish Religion and Politics

Pharisees. After returning to Jerusalem, there was a conservative movement that believed if the people of God would follow the Deuteronomy Covenant, then God would send His Messiah. The Pharisees were a group of religious leaders who believed this. The problem was that in addition to keeping the laws of God, they added their own laws. They took pride in their human efforts to keep their extra set of laws and eventually considered their laws more important than God's.

Ironically, Jesus of Nazareth would have most closely resembled the conservative teaching regarding keeping God's laws. In addition, the Pharisees were supporters of the rabbinical system of discipleship. For this reason, Jesus was a bit of a paradox to the Pharisees. In their minds, God was required to send the Messiah based on his promise to bless God's people if they followed His laws. As a result, the Pharisees believed that the Messiah would credit his arrival to their efforts.

Jesus claimed to be the Messiah. He did powerful supernatural miracles. But rather than thanking the Pharisees, He rebuked them. Rather than praising the Pharisees, Jesus called out their hypocrisy.

Sadducees. In contrast to the Pharisees, the Sadducees were wealthy, powerful, and politically connected. Instead of attempting to closely follow God's laws like the Pharisees, the Sadducees believed that relief from the Romans would occur by embracing the secular Greek forms of Government, culture, and thought. As a result, they rejected the majority of the Hebrew Scriptures, including the idea that God would raise people from the dead. This becomes a crucial item during the trial of Paul.

Sanhedrin. With the influence of the temple waning and no Jewish King to sit on a throne, the Sanhedrin was considered the Jewish system of Government and law. Made up of 70 men and led by the High Priest, there were both Pharisees and Sadducees on the counsel.
Herodians. As their name implies, the Herodians were supporters of Herod. More closely aligned with Sadducees, the Herodians were the political group who desired to gain wealth and power by being closely aligned with those who occupied their country.

Zealots. In contrast to the Herodians who embraced compromise, the Zealots were a political group that would have been more closely aligned with the Pharisees. They believed that it was going to be physical force and violence that would ultimately remove the Romans. From their perspective, when the Messiah arrived, then he would be a military man like Joshua, Gideon, or David in the Old Testament, and a military leader would need people to fight. The Zealots were the ones looking for the fight. On of the disciples of Jesus Christ was himself a zealot.

Learn to Read like a Detective

Close Readers

1. Read the text slowly at least three times.
2. Circle words that they are unsure of and try to figure them out.
3. Reread, annotate, underline key concepts or vocabulary.
4. Summarize or answer specific questions

Reading 1.

- Who are the *characters*?
- What is the *setting*?
- What is the *problem*?
- *Highlight* the important parts.
- Mark anything you notice that is important
- Think; what is this text about?

Reading 2.

- Gain additional understanding considering the overall context.
- Ask questions and make additional observations.
- Circle anything you do not understand.
- Mark anything else that you notice that is important.
- Think. Explain the marks that you made.

Reading 3.

- Read the Essential Question(s).
- Reread the text to identify evidence that answers the question.
- Make inferences.
- Make connections.
- Make application.
- Write your answer.
- Cite your source in the text.

Use Sticky Notes to...

- Highlight an interesting part
- Ask a question that you want to come back to
- Make a written connection to another text or passage.
- Highlight a word, concept, or question that you don't understand.
- Record personal thoughts, reflections or prayers resulting from your interaction with the text.
- Sketch a drawing or a symbol that helps you think about what you read or are learning.

Paul Appears before Festus

Acts 25:122

Three days after Festus arrived in Caesarea to take over his new responsibilities, he left for Jerusalem, 2 where the leading priests and other Jewish leaders met with him and made their accusations against Paul. 3 They asked Festus as a favor to transfer Paul to Jerusalem (planning to ambush and kill him on the way).
4 But Festus replied that Paul was at Caesarea and he himself would be returning there soon.
5 So he said, "Those of you in authority can return with me. If Paul has done anything wrong, you can make your accusations."
6 About eight or ten days later Festus returned to Caesarea, and on the following day he took his seat in court and ordered that Paul be brought in. 7 When Paul arrived, the Jewish leaders from Jerusalem gathered around and made many serious accusations they couldn't prove.
8 Paul denied the charges. "I am not guilty of any crime against the Jewish laws or the Temple or the Roman government," he said.
9 Then Festus, wanting to please the Jews, asked him, "Are you willing to go to Jerusalem and stand trial before me there?"
10 But Paul replied, "No! This is the official Roman court, so I ought to be tried right here. You know very well I am not guilty of harming the Jews. 11 If I have done something worthy of death, I don't refuse to die. But if I am innocent, no one has a right to turn me over to these men to kill me. I appeal to Caesar!"
12 Festus conferred with his advisers and then replied, "Very well! You have appealed to Caesar, and to Caesar you will go!"
13 A few days later King Agrippa arrived with his sister, Bernice, to pay their respects to Festus. 14 During their stay of several days, Festus discussed Paul's case with the king. "There is a prisoner here," he told him, "whose case was left for me by Felix. 15 When I was in Jerusalem, the leading priests and Jewish elders pressed charges against him and asked me to condemn him. 16 I pointed out to them that Roman law does not convict people without a trial. They must be given an opportunity to confront their accusers and defend themselves.
17 "When his accusers came here for the trial, I didn't delay. I called the case the very next day and ordered Paul brought in. 18 But the accusations made against him weren't any of the crimes I expected. 19 Instead, it was something about their religion and a dead man named Jesus, who Paul insists is alive. 20 I was at a loss to know how to investigate these things, so I asked him whether he would be willing to stand trial on these charges in Jerusalem. 21 But Paul appealed to have his case decided by the emperor. So I ordered that he be held in custody until I could arrange to send him to Caesar."
22 "I'd like to hear the man myself," Agrippa said.
And Festus replied, "You will–tomorrow!"

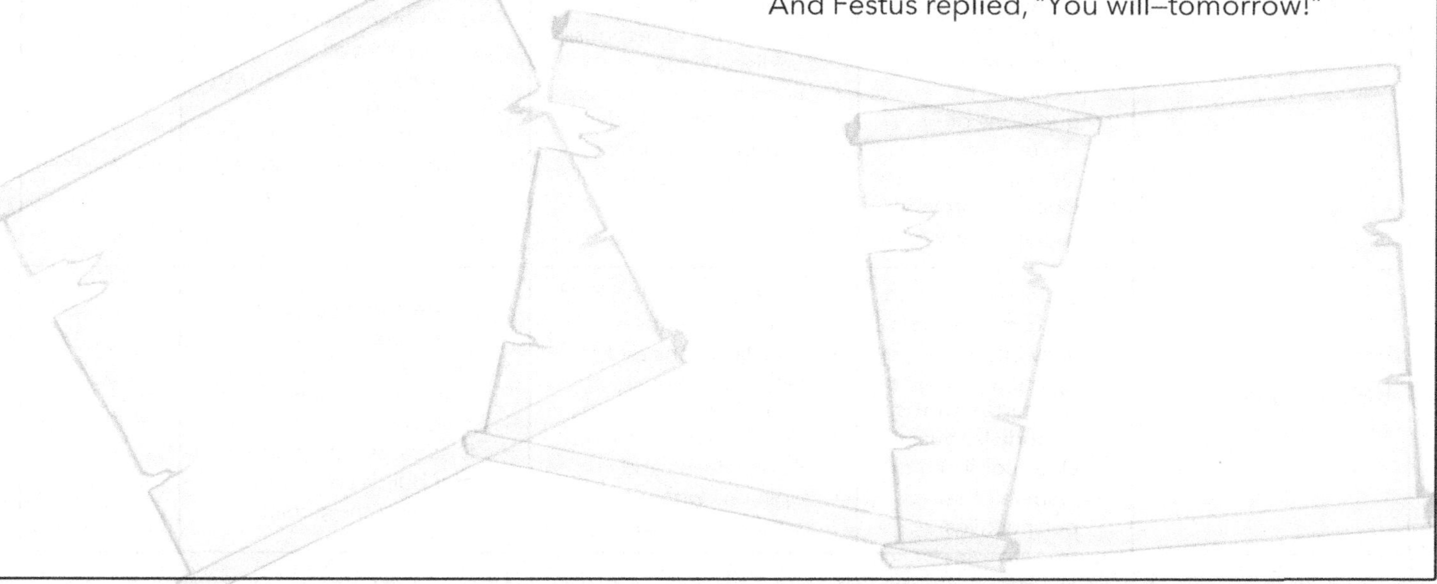

Detective Evaluation

<table>
<tr><th colspan="5">COLLABORATION RUBRIC</th></tr>
<tr><td colspan="5">Notes and Plans:
</td></tr>
<tr><th></th><th>Below Standard</th><th>Approaching Standard</th><th>At Standard</th><th>Above Standard</th></tr>
<tr><td>Takes Personal Responsibility for Learning and Contributing to the Learning Process</td><td>• Is not prepared, informed or ready to contribute to the team
• Does not utilize technology as agreed upon
• Does not participate in project tasks
• Does not listen to or use feedback to improve work</td><td>• Usually prepared, informed and ready to work with team
• Does not utilize technology according to agreed upon standards with consistency
• Needs reminding or prompting to complete tasks
• Uses some feedback and complete most tasks</td><td>• Prepared and ready to work
• Well informed and cites evidence that encourages learning among other team members
• Consistently uses technology as agree upon
• Self motivated and does not need to be reminded to complete tasks
• Completes tasks on time
• Evaluates and uses feedback to improve work</td><td></td></tr>
<tr><td>Contribution to the Team</td><td>• Does not help the team to solve problems; may be the source of problems for the team
• Does not ask probing questions, express ideas, or elaborate in response to questions or discussions
• Do not offer help
• Does not provide useful feedback</td><td>• Cooperates but does not actively participate in problem solving
• Occasionally asks probing questions, expresses ideas, or elaborates in responses or discussions
• Sometimes offers help
• Sometimes provides feedback but it may not always be helpful</td><td>• Helps the team to solve problems and manage conflict
• Clearly expresses ideas, asks probing questions, listens to others and solicits feedback from quiet team members to ensure that all perspectives are shared and heard
• Provides useful feedback
• Identifies opportunities to help others where appropriate</td><td></td></tr>
<tr><td>Relationships and Respect</td><td>• Impolite or unkind to team members (may interrupt, ignore, talk over or use hurtful words or body language)
• Does not listen or respect other perspectives</td><td>• Usually polite and kind to team members
• Usually listens and respects team members
• Disagrees with content, perspectives and opinions without attacking the person</td><td>• Polite and kind to team members
• Listens to, acknowledges and respects other team members
• Disagrees with content and builds community by affirming the person</td><td></td></tr>
</table>

TRUE HERO

"The true story of the extraordinary mission of God"

prologue

Learning to love God's Word

For we did not follow cleverly devised stories when we told you about the coming of our Lord Jesus Christ in power, but we were *eyewitnesses* of his majesty.

2 Peter 1:16 (NIV)

For we did not follow cleverly devised myths when we made known to you the power and coming of our Lord Jesus Christ, but we were *eyewitnesses* of his majesty.

2 Peter 1:16 (ESV)

For we have not followed cunningly devised fables, when we made known unto you the power and coming of our Lord Jesus Christ, but were *eyewitnesses* of his majesty.

2 Peter 1:16 (KJV)

The investigation begins...

In Acts 25, we read that Paul appears before Festus. First, his accusers make their accusations against him.

Then Paul is allowed the opportunity to defend himself against the charges that he is accused of.

The problem is that the Jewish leaders were unable to prove their accusations against Paul. They did not have any evidence.

Because they did not have any evidence, it became the word of Paul against those who were accusing him.

Ask an attorney what they would like to have in order to help ensure a conviction, and they will most likely tell you two things.

First, they will tell you that they would like to have a credible eyewitness.

A credible eyewitness is a person who objectively saw the events that took place and can tell their story with integrity.

Paul before Festus

Acts 25:7 When Paul arrived, the Jewish leaders from Jerusalem gathered around and made many serious accusations they couldn't prove.

8 Paul denied the charges. "I am not guilty of any crime against the Jewish laws or the Temple or the Roman government," he said.

This person is credible because they have nothing to gain by telling the truth. In fact, many times, they place themselves in a position of risk or danger if they tell the truth.

The second thing that they will say is that they would love to have unique, credible evidence that proves beyond a reasonable doubt that the individual who is accused of the crime is the one who committed the crime.

For example, finding a fingerprint or some other unique identifier that could only belong to that individual. In many ways, the prophecies from the Hebrew Scriptures were so specific and unique that they act like fingerprints.

In this part of the investigation, we will examine the credibility of the eyewitness and then compare their testimony regarding the life of Christ with the Hebrew prophecies to determine if the evidence (fingerprints) are enough to convict Christ of being the Messiah.

Who were the eyewitnesses, and can we trust them?

> *"When his (Paul's) accusers came here for the trial, I didn't delay. I called the case the very next day and ordered Paul brought in.*
> *But the accusations made against him weren't any of the crimes I expected. Instead, it was something about their religion and a dead man named Jesus, who Paul insists is alive.*
> *I was at a loss to know how to investigate these things, so I asked him whether he would be willing to stand trial on these charges in Jerusalem.*
>
> *Governor Festus*
> *Acts 26:17-20*

CAN WE TRUST THE CREDIBILITY OF THE EYEWITNESSES?

During his defense, Paul admits to being a follower of "the Way" and makes several claims about a man by the name of Jesus of Nazareth.

The followers of the Way believed that Jesus was the Messiah that was promised to the descendants of the children of Abraham, Isaac, and Jacob through the prophets of Israel.

During this first part of our investigation, you will be examining the prophecies about the promised Messiah and comparing them with the eyewitness accounts of the life of Jesus Christ.

> "I admit that I follow the Way, which they call a cult. I worship the God of our ancestors, and I firmly believe the Jewish law, and everything written in the prophets.
>
> Paul
> Acts 26:14

While there are many eyewitnesses, there are four that we will be concentrating on during this part of the investigation.

Your goal is to ensure that the witnesses are credible and then to check to see if the evidence supports that Jesus fulfilled the prophecies and could be the Messiah that people claim he is.

Who were the eyewitnesses, and can we trust them?

Breaking the silence...

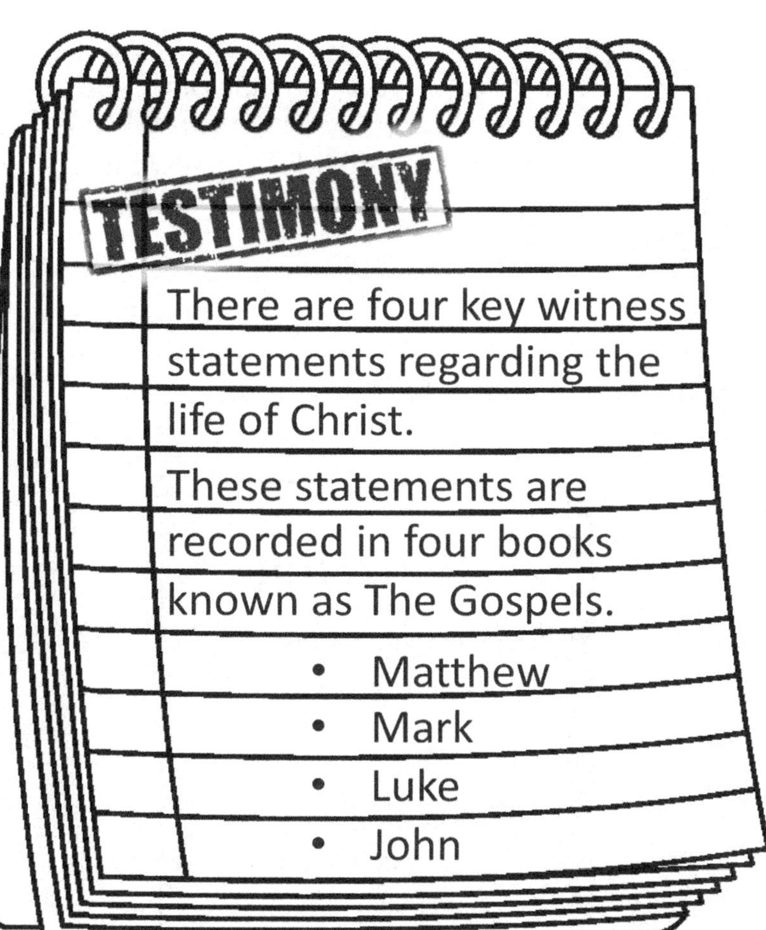

The word Gospel simply means Good News. After 400 years, God broke His silence with the proclamation that the Messiah was on His way.

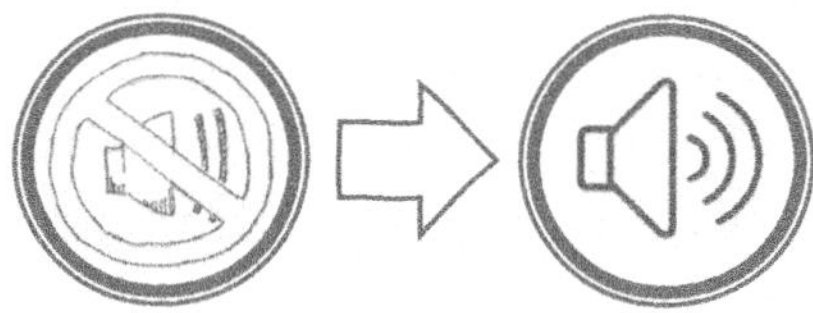

For the people of God, this was Good News! The one who was chosen and anointed by God to deliver His people would finally arrive.

The various announcements are recorded in each of the Gospels along with the life, death, and resurrection of Christ.

But how do we know we can believe these accounts? Are we positive that the Gospels that bear the names of Matthew, Mark, Luke, and John were written by the men who are credited with the work?

Who were the eyewitnesses, and can we trust them?

Are the Gospel writers credible?

Can scholars guarantee with 100% certainty that the authors of the Gospels were Matthew, Mark, Luke, and John?

In a word, no.

But does that mean that we should disregard the Gospels or perhaps more importantly, does it mean that there is not overwhelming evidence to make an educated guess (inference) that

Don't Forget!

A good detective checks all their sources and decides if they are reliable witnesses.

Matthew

The testimony of the leaders of the early church unanimously accepted the idea that Matthew was the author of the gospel that bears his name.

Matthew was a tax collector and one of the 12 disciples of Jesus Christ. Matthew would have been well educated, have an attention to detail, and be very familiar both with the Hebrew Scriptures as well as the day to day life of Christ. Matthew is written from a Jewish perspective to a Jewish audience. In addition to providing eyewitness testimony, the Gospel of Matthew has more references and inferences to Hebrew individuals, events, and prophecies than the other gospels.

One of the primary goals of Matthew is to inform the Hebrew people that God fulfilled His promise and that their distinctively Jewish Messiah had arrived. Irenaeus, an influential leader of the church during the second century, confirms that Matthew is the author of this book.

Inferences

Authors may hint at an idea without stating it directly.

You must use what you already know about a topic to make a connection and figure out what is being communicated.

- You make an inference by combining text clues with your background knowledge to arrive at a logical conclusion or an "educated guess."

Sourcing

Before reading a text ask...

- Who wrote this?
- What is the perspective of the author?
- When was it written?
- Where was it written?
- Is it reliable?
    - Why or Why not?

Who were the eyewitnesses, and can we trust them?

The Gospel According to Matthew

Matthew begins his account of the life of Jesus by demonstrating that Jesus is qualified to be the Messiah through His genealogy.

Matthew begins with Abraham and shows how Jesus is the one who is the promised lion from the tribe of Judah and the one who was promised to David to be the King of Kings.

Copies of the text of Matthew found in Qumran lead scholars to believe that Matthew was originally written in Hebrew.

One of the cool things that Matthew does with his account of the life of Christ can be found in the early chapters where Matthew goes out of his way to demonstrate the connection between the Hebrew Scriptures, the histories of the patriarchs, and the events in the life of Christ.

Matthew demonstrates how Jesus was...

- Born of a woman who should not have been able to have a child;
- Born of a woman whose Hebrew name was Miriam;
- Born of a man named Joseph, who had several dreams including one that instructed him to take his family down to Egypt;
- Born at a time when a tyrannical ruler was killing all the Hebrew babies;
- Had his life preserved in Egypt;
- Was baptized in the Jordan river at the exact same spot Joshua would have crossed the Jordan before entering the land God had promised;
- Spent 40 days in the wilderness being tempted;
- And many more ...

The first miracle that Matthew records from the life of Christ also sends a significant message to his primarily Jewish audience.

Matthew waits until the 8th chapter before mentioning a specific miracle performed by Jesus. This is significant for several reasons.

First, Matthew focuses on demonstrating how Christ fulfills the qualifications of the Messiah.

Second, one of the ways that Matthew accomplishes his goal is by recording 5 specific discourses (lengthy teachings) of Christ. This is done as a reminder to the Jewish audience of the first 5 books of the Hebrew Scriptures.

Third, the miracle that Matthew records is the cleansing of a leper. This is significant because in the minds of his Jewish audience leprosy was viewed as a punishment for sin.

Look at the interaction between Christ and the leper and you can see the message Matthew was communicating to Israel; if they would just kneel before their Messiah, He was willing to cleans them and take away the sin of the people.

> When Jesus came down from the mountainside, large crowds followed him. 2 A man with leprosy came and knelt before him and said, "Lord, if you are willing, you can make me clean."
> 3 Jesus reached out his hand and touched the man. "I am willing," he said.
> "Be clean!" Immediately he was cleansed of his leprosy.
>
> Matthew 8:1-3

Who were the eyewitnesses, and can we trust them?

The Gospels According to Mark and Luke

Mark

Evidence suggests that the Gospel of Mark was the earliest written gospel.

Scholars believe that it was written between AD 55-70 before the destruction of Herod's Temple in Jerusalem in AD 70.

The same early church leader Irenaeus who testifies to the credibility of the Gospel of Matthew spoke about how Peter and Paul were together in Rome preaching the Gospel.

It is believed that occurred just before the death of Peter in the early to mid-60's.

The reason that this is significant is that a close reading of Mark also suggests that Peter is the primary source for the Gospel account.

One of the things that makes Mark unique is the poor grammar that is evident within the text. Remember that Peter is referred to as an uneducated fisherman and it is evident from Mark's writing style that he lacked higher levels of education as well.

Mark was not one of the original 12 disciples. He is mentioned in the book of Acts as one of the companions of Paul and Barnabas which means that he would have also been in close relationship with Dr. Luke who was Paul's personal physician.

So it makes sense to conclude that Mark, written from the personal reflections of Peter would have been one of the people who Luke references as being one of the people he consulted during his "careful research."

Luke

Like Mark, Luke was not one of the original 12 disciples of Jesus either. Instead, he a doctor who was a close companion of Paul and served on Paul's missionary team.

He writes what he claims is a carefully researched account of the life of Christ followed by the book of Acts which is the historical account of the early church.

While he may not have been an eyewitness, as a companion of Paul he would have had direct contact with Peter, John, and the other disciples during their shared time in Jerusalem and Rome.

What makes the Gospel of Luke significant, as well as unique, is that unlike Mark who demonstrates more of a common usage of the Greek language, Luke uses words that are specific to physicians and the medical field at that time.

In addition, Luke records more of Christ's miracles than any other Gospel and more of Christ's interactions with women than any other gospel.

This suggests that while Peter and Mark had more "cut to the chase" personality types, Luke viewed the life and ministry of Christ through the eyes of a physician with a caring and gracious bedside manner.

Writing with a polytheistic Greek audience in mind, the first miracle recorded by Dr. Luke was the casting out of a demon. Instead of tracing the genealogy of Christ through Joseph back to Abraham, Luke traces the genealogy through Mary back to Adam as the father of all mankind.

Who were the eyewitnesses, and can we trust them?

The Gospels According to John

John

Matthew, Mark, and Luke are referred to as the synoptic Gospels because they are so similar.

In contrast, over 90 percent of John's Gospel records different events than the other three.

John, known as the disciple whom Jesus loved is believed to be the youngest of the 12 disciples and in his early teens at the time of the life and ministry of Christ.

John, who also authored three short letters that bear his name as well as the book of Revelation, would spend his last years on the Greek Island of Patmos.

Perhaps is was this proximity to Greek culture and the Greek way of thinking that influenced John's desire to demonstrate how Christ was not only the Messiah to the Jews but also the Gentiles.

John's gospel is poetic and beautiful. It makes equal inferences to the Jewish Tabernacle as well as to Plato's allegory of the cave.

John ends his Gospel with the mission statement that "these are written that you (the reader) might believe that Jesus is the Christ, the Son of God."

Read like a Detective

Paul claims that Jesus of Nazareth meets the requirements to be the promised Jewish Messiah. Your job is to investigate the claim.

Part 1. Examine the Witness statements and summarize the evidence.

Part 2. There are a group of Essene scribes outside of Jerusalem in Qumran who are making copies of the Hebrew Scriptures. Go to Qumran and examine the Hebrew prophecies about the Messiah. Then compare and contrast the prophecies with the eyewitness testimony and decide for yourself if Jesus fulfilled the prophecies.

Detective Skills

For this investigation you will need to examine the evidence and make inferences.

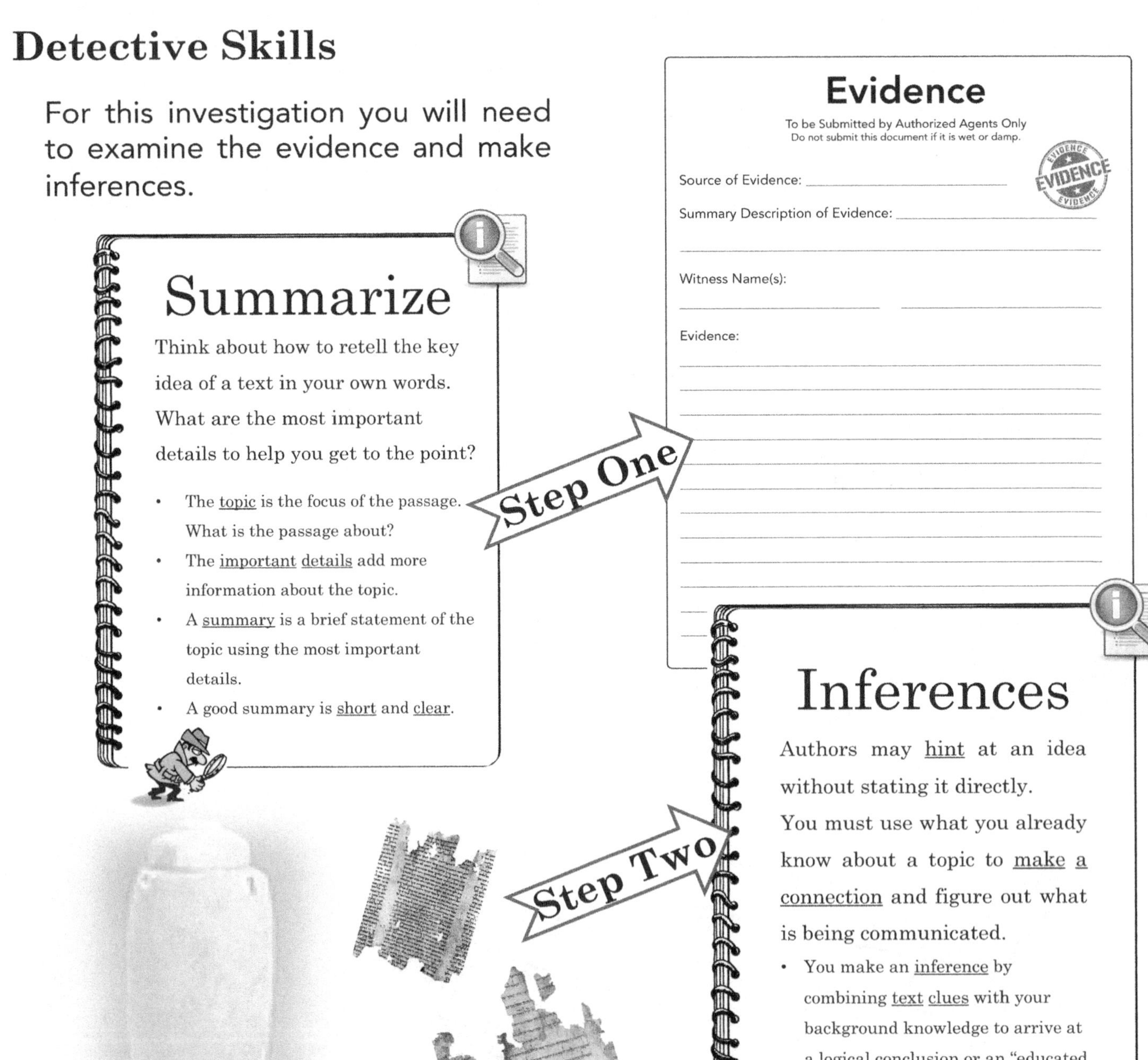

Read like a Detective

- Read the witness statement.
- Summarize the evidence.
- Do not forget to cite the evidence in your notes so that you can identify it later.

Witness Statement

Matthew, Former Tax Collector, Disciple of Jesus the Nazarene

Matthew 2:16-18

Matthew 26:15, 27:5-7

Matthew 27:35

1. **Collect evidence.**
2. **Read like a detective.**
3. **Preserve the evidence.**
4. Evaluate the evidence.
5. Cite the evidence.

Read like a Detective

- Read the witness statement.
- Summarize the Evidence.
- Do not forget to cite the evidence in your notes so that you can identify it later.

Witness Statement

Mark, companion of Peter the Disciple and a part of Paull's missionary team

1. **Collect evidence.**
2. **Read like a detective.**
3. **Preserve the evidence.**
4. Evaluate the evidence.
5. Cite the evidence.

Read like a Detective
1. Collect evidence.
2. Read like a detective.
3. Preserve the evidence.
4. Evaluate the evidence.
5. Cite the evidence.
Luke 1:26-27, 30-31
Luke 2:4-7
Luke 3:33
Luke 1:32-33
Witness Statement
Dr. Luke, Physician, Companion of Paul

Investigate like a Detective

- Go to the caves in Qumran where the Essenes are copying the Scriptures.
- Evaluate the manuscripts to determine the correct references.
- Summarize the evidence from the Hebrew prophets.
- Do not forget to cite the evidence in your notes so that you can identify it later.

1. **Collect evidence.**
2. **Read like a detective.**
3. **Preserve the evidence.**
4. Evaluate the evidence.
5. Cite the evidence.

Isaiah 9:

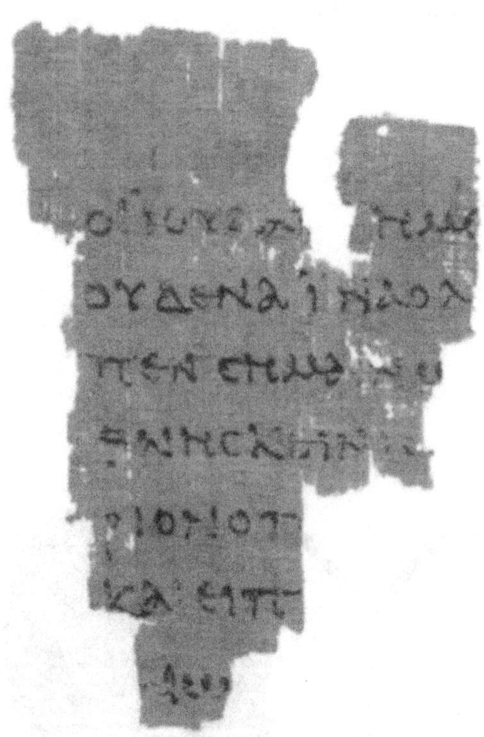

P52, a papyrus fragment from a codex (c. 90–160), one of the earliest known New Testament manuscripts.

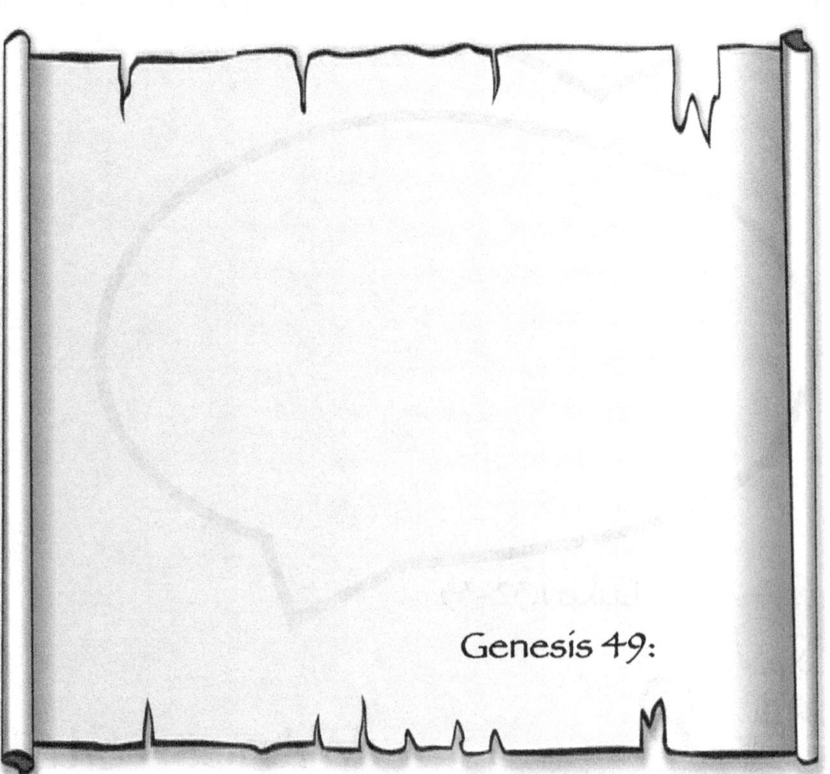

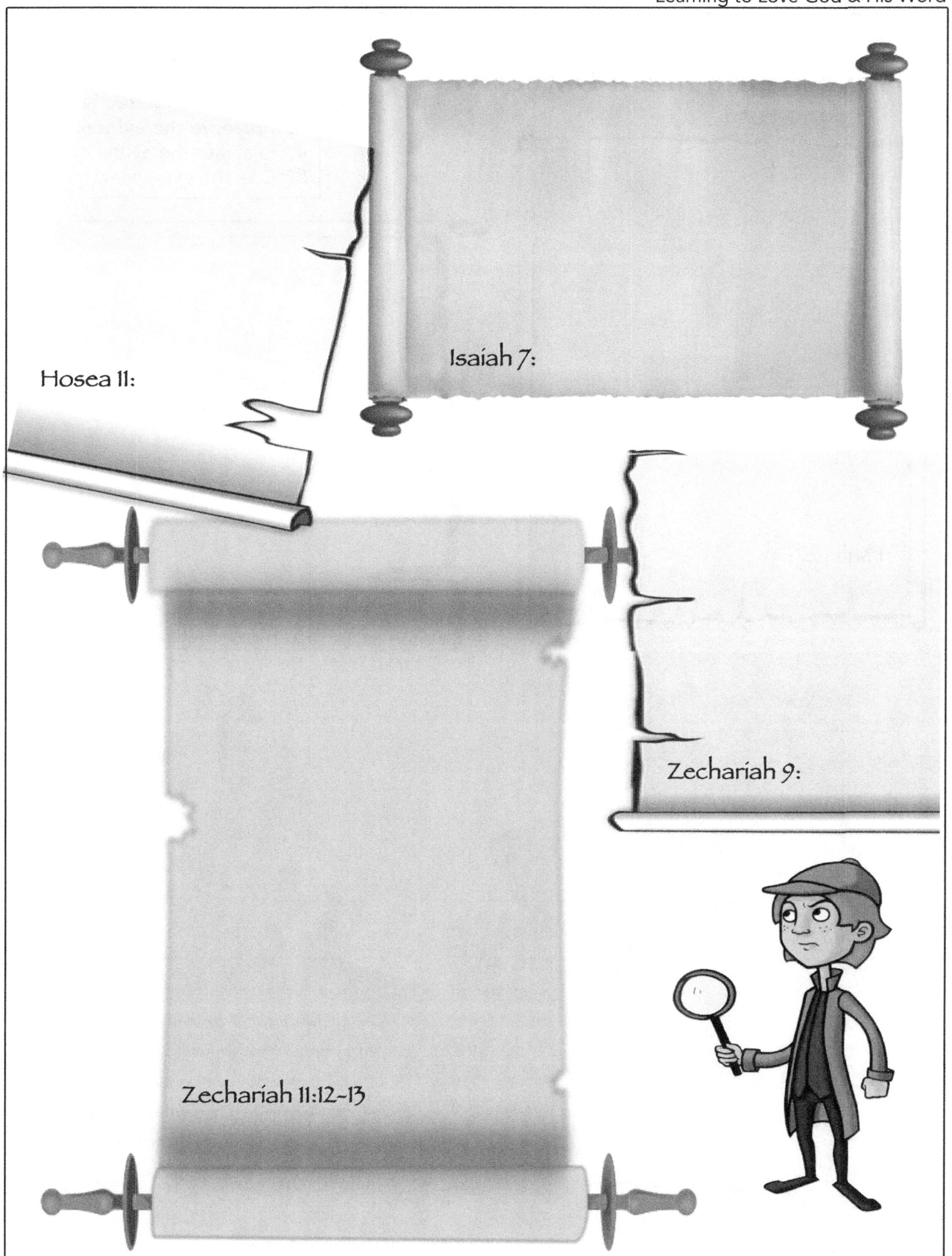
Isaiah 7:
Hosea 11:
Zechariah 9:
Zechariah 11:12-13

Investigate like a Detective

1. **Collect evidence.**
2. **Read like a detective.**
3. **Preserve the evidence.**
4. Evaluate the evidence.
5. Cite the evidence.

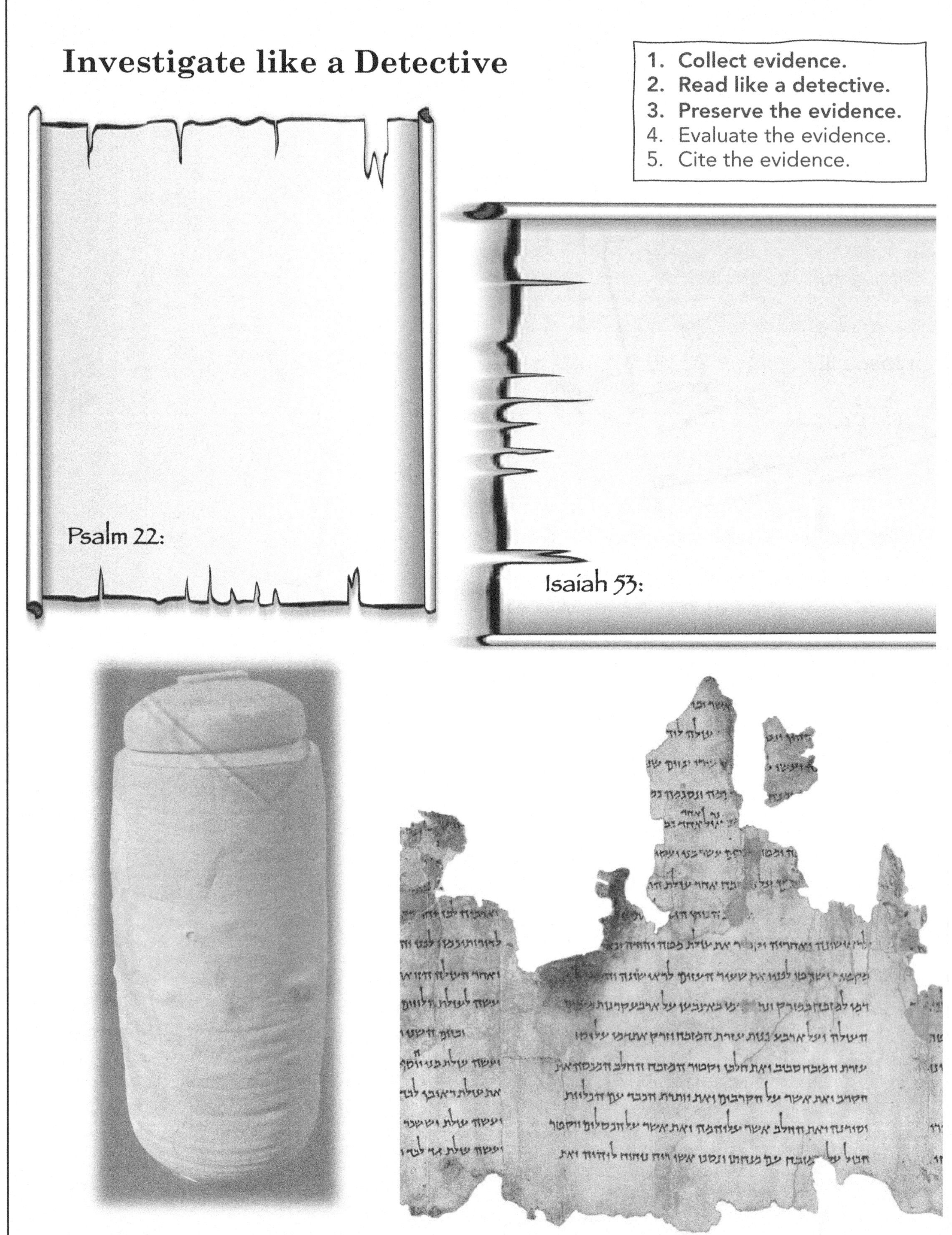

Investigate like a Detective

1. **Collect evidence.**
2. **Read like a detective.**
3. **Preserve the evidence.**
4. Evaluate the evidence.
5. Cite the evidence.

Psalm 16:10, 49:15

Evaluate like a Detective

The evidence board

Is Paul's claim correct? Does Jesus meet the requirements to be the prophesied Messiah?

1. Collect evidence.
2. Read like a detective.
3. Preserve the evidence.
4. **Evaluate the evidence**.
5. Cite the evidence.

Evidence Board

Inferences

Authors may <u>hint</u> at an idea without stating it directly.

You must use what you already know about a topic to <u>make a connection</u> and figure out what is being communicated.

- You make an <u>inference</u> by combining <u>text clues</u> with your background knowledge to arrive at a <u>logical conclusion</u> or an "<u>educated guess</u>."

Evidence

To be Submitted by Authorized Agents Only
Do not submit this document if it is wet or damp.

Source of Evidence: ______________________________

Summary Description of Evidence: ______________________________

Witness Reference(s):	Qumran Evidence:
______________________________	______________________________
______________________________	______________________________
______________________________	______________________________
______________________________	______________________________
______________________________	______________________________
______________________________	______________________________
______________________________	______________________________
______________________________	______________________________
______________________________	______________________________

Evidence Summary:

____

____

____

Evaluate like a Detective

What are your conclusions?

Is Paul's claim correct? Does Jesus meet the requirements to be the prophesied Messiah?

Project Response

- What are 2 or 3 things that challenge your thinking?
- How does this project impact your perspective of Jesus the Nazarene?

Notes:

Investigation Summary

To be Submitted by Authorized Agents Only
Do not submit this document if it is wet or damp.

EVIDENCE

Source of Evidence: ______________________________

Summary Description of Evidence:

____

____

____

____

____

____

____

____

____

____

____

____

____

____

____

____

____

____

Mission Report

EVIDENCE

CLASSIFIED

Detective Evaluation

COLLABORATION RUBRIC

Notes and Plans:

	Below Standard	Approaching Standard	At Standard	Above Standard
Takes Personal Responsibility for Learning and Contributing to the Learning Process	• Is not prepared, informed or ready to contribute to the team • Does not utilize technology as agreed upon • Does not participate in project tasks • Does not listen to or use feedback to improve work	• Usually prepared, informed and ready to work with team • Does not utilize technology according to agreed upon standards with consistency • Needs reminding or prompting to complete tasks • Uses some feedback and complete most tasks	• Prepared and ready to work • Well informed and cites evidence that encourages learning among other team members • Consistently uses technology as agree upon • Self motivated and does not need to be reminded to complete tasks • Completes tasks on time • Evaluates and uses feedback to improve work	
Contribution to the Team	• Does not help the team to solve problems; may be the source of problems for the team • Does not ask probing questions, express ideas, or elaborate in response to questions or discussions • Do not offer help • Does not provide useful feedback	• Cooperates but does not actively participate in problem solving • Occasionally asks probing questions, expresses ideas, or elaborates in responses or discussions • Sometimes offers help • Sometimes provides feedback but it may not always be helpful	• Helps the team to solve problems and manage conflict • Clearly expresses ideas, asks probing questions, listens to others and solicits feedback from quiet team members to ensure that all perspectives are shared and heard • Provides useful feedback • Identifies opportunities to help others where appropriate	
Relationships and Respect	• Impolite or unkind to team members (may interrupt, ignore, talk over or use hurtful words or body language) • Does not listen or respect other perspectives	• Usually polite and kind to team members • Usually listens and respects team members • Disagrees with content, perspectives and opinions without attacking the person	• Polite and kind to team members • Listens to, acknowledges and respects other team members • Disagrees with content and builds community by affirming the person	

TRUE HERO

"The true story of the extraordinary mission of God"

★★★★★

patriarch

Learning to love God's Word

In the same region there were some shepherds staying out in the fields and keeping watch over their flock by night. And an angel of the Lord suddenly stood before them, and the glory of the Lord shone around them; and they were terribly frightened. But the angel said to them, "Do not be afraid; for behold, I bring you good news of great joy which will be for all the people; for today in the city of David there has been born for you a Savior, who is Christ the Lord. This will be a sign for you: you will find a baby wrapped in cloths and lying in a manger." And suddenly there appeared with the angel a multitude of the heavenly host praising God and saying,.

"Glory to God in the highest, And on earth peace among men with whom He is pleased."

Luke 2:8-14

Who was Jesus the Nazarene, and did He claim to be the Messiah?

Were the miracles of Jesus real? Did He claim to be God

At the center of Paul's defense is the person of Jesus Christ.

At the time of his birth the Jewish people were eager for God to fulfill His promise and send His Messiah to rescue Israel.

One of those who was eagerly waiting was a man by the name of Simeon. The Gospel writer Luke, who writes from the experience of Mary (the mother of Jesus) tells us about what happened a few days after Christ was born.

At that time there was a man in Jerusalem named Simeon. He was righteous and devout and was eagerly waiting for the Messiah to come and rescue Israel. The Holy Spirit was upon him and had revealed to him that he would not die until he had seen the Lord's Messiah.

That day the Spirit led him to the Temple. So when Mary and Joseph came to present the baby Jesus to the Lord as the law required, Simeon was there. He took the child in his arms and praised God, saying,

"Sovereign Lord, now let your servant die in peace,
as you have promised.
I have seen your salvation,
which you have prepared for all people.
He is a light to reveal God to the nations,
and he is the glory of your people Israel!"

Luke 2:25-32

Clue. What's in a name?

Jesus

- In Hebrew, the name **Jesus** is the name Yeshua.
- ***Yeshua*** is the name for Joshua in the Hebrew Scriptures.
- ***Joshua*** means: YWH, God is salvation.
- In Act I, Joshua crosses the Jordan river and delivers the people into the Promised Land.
- Joshua also conquers and settles the people into the land.
- Throughout Scripture when you read the word, "salvation" you are most likely reading the word, "Yeshua" which is the literal name given to Jesus.
- So in this instance, Simeon declares, "I have seen your Yeshua!"
- In other words, *"I have seen the deliverance of God."*

Did Jesus claim to be the Messiah?

In a trial or an investigation it is important to examine all of the evidence and all of the eyewitnesses to determine the truth.

One of the most important eyewitnesses in any trial is the person who is on trial.

In our case, Paul is on trial but a key to his defense is that Jesus of Nazareth is the Jewish Messiah.

So it is important to our investigation to determine whether Jesus claimed to be the Messiah or if He believed that He was the Messiah.

To do that we need to examine what Jesus said and what Jesus did.

In this part of our investigation we will be examining eyewitness accounts of the the claims that Christ makes about Himself.

According to eyewitnesses, Jesus the Nazarene does not simply claim to be telling the truth, Jesus claims that He is truth.

"I am the way and the truth and the life. No one comes to the Father except through me."

John 14:6

Is Jesus the Christ?

Many individuals have claimed that they are the Messiah that God has promised.

Even Jesus warned people that many would come and make false claims (Matthew 24:24).

But what does it mean to "be the Messiah?"

The word Messiah is a title, not a name.

Comparable to how we would use the title Doctor, or Mr. or Mrs., to formally address someone, we would use the word Messiah as a title to recognize the role of Messiah.

The title Messiah refers to the person who is promised by God to be the one who delivers God's people.

Throughout the plot of the Old Testament there are many individuals that God appoints to deliver His people. Moses, Joshua, the Judges, David, and others.

The people of Israel were expecting someone like one of these examples. They were expecting a Joshua (Yeshua) or a David who would raise and army and drive out the Roman soldiers from their land.

But instead of meeting their expectations, Jesus (Yeshua) died a shameful death on a cross.

The word Messiah is Hebrew but remember that by the time of Jesus the Hebrew Scriptures had been translated into the Greek Septuagint.

The Greek translation of Messiah is Christ. That is why when Andrew tells his brother Peter that they have found the Christ, he is saying that they have found the Messiah (John 1:41).

Did Jesus claim to be the Messiah?

The disciple John, ends his gospel by stating that his purpose in writing was that his readers might believe that Jesus is the Christ, the Son of God, and that through their belief they may experience life in His name (John 20:31)

Paul, believed that Jesus was the Christ. John believed that Jesus was the Christ. Andrew told His brother Peter that he had found the Christ.

But did Jesus believe that He was the Christ?

"***Christ***" is the connecting point within the plot of Scripture.

The promise and the arrival of the ***Messiah*** is the connection between the Testaments.

What happened at Jacob's well?

Jesus and the disciples had just left Jerusalem and were heading back home to Galilee. On the way they take a detour and stop and Jacob's Well.

Jacob's well is an important place geographically in Israel.

Multiple significant events happen at that location.

It is the place where Abraham made the first sacrifice in the land of Israel.

It is also close to Shechem where most of the book of Deuteronomy took place.

In John 4, it is the place where Jesus meets and talks with a Samaritan woman.

Symbolically this is significant on many different levels.

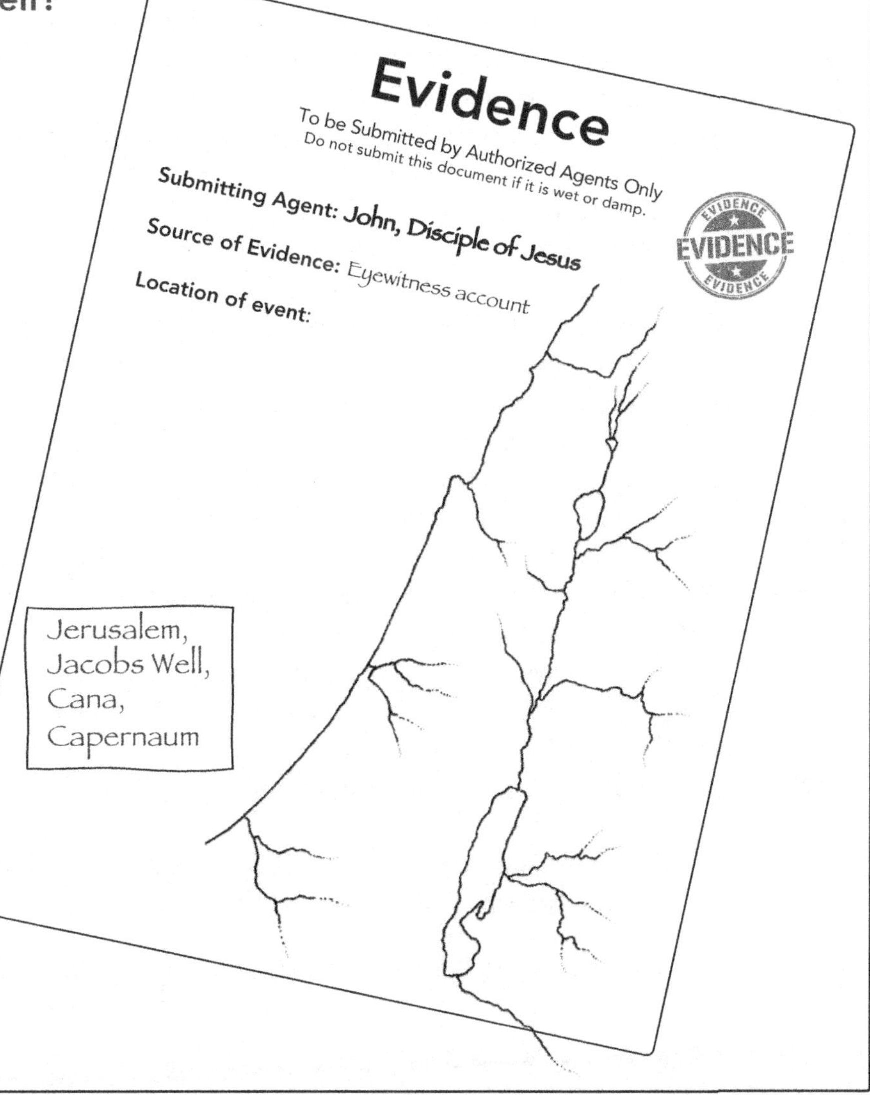

The Testimony of John
The Disciple of Jesus the Nazarene
Recorded in John 4

Now Jesus learned that the Pharisees had heard that he was gaining and
baptizing more disciples than John— 2 although in fact it was not Jesus who
baptized, but his disciples. 3 So he left Judea and went back once more to Galilee.
4 Now he had to go through Samaria. 5 So he came to a town in Samaria called
Sychar, near the plot of ground Jacob had given to his son Joseph. 6 Jacob's well
was there, and Jesus, tired as he was from the journey, sat down by the well. It
was about noon.
7 When a Samaritan woman came to draw water, Jesus said to her,
"Will you give me a drink?" 8 (His disciples had gone into the town to buy food.)
9 The Samaritan woman said to him, "You are a Jew and I am a Samaritan woman.
How can you ask me for a drink?" (For Jews do not associate with Samaritans.)
10 Jesus answered her, "If you knew the gift of God and who it is that asks you for
a drink, you would have asked him, and he would have given you living water."
11 "Sir," the woman said, "you have nothing to draw with and the well is deep.
Where can you get this living water? 12 Are you greater than our father Jacob, who
gave us the well and drank from it himself, as did also his sons and his livestock?"
13 Jesus answered, "Everyone who drinks this water will be thirsty again, 14 but
whoever drinks the water I give them will never thirst. Indeed, the water I give them
will become in them a spring of water welling up to eternal life."
15 The woman said to him, "Sir, give me this water so that I won't get thirsty and
have to keep coming here to draw water."
16 He told her, "Go, call your husband and come back."
17 "I have no husband," she replied.
Jesus said to her, "You are right when you say you have no husband. 18 The fact
is, you have had five husbands, and the man you now have is not your husband.
What you have just said is quite true."
19 "Sir," the woman said, "I can see that you are a prophet. 20 Our ancestors
worshiped on this mountain, but you Jews claim that the place where we must
worship is in Jerusalem."
21 "Woman," Jesus replied, "believe me, a time is coming when you will worship the
Father neither on this mountain nor in Jerusalem. 22 You Samaritans worship what
you do not know; we worship what we do know, for salvation is from the
Jews. 23 Yet a time is coming and has now come when the true worshipers will
worship the Father in the Spirit and in truth, for they are the kind of
worshipers the Father seeks. 24 God is spirit, and his worshipers must worship
in the Spirit and in truth."

25 The woman said, "I know that Messiah" (called Christ) "is coming. When he
comes, he will explain everything to us."

26 Then Jesus declared, "I, the one speaking to you—I am he."

Detective Notes:

The word Messiah means "one chosen and *anointed* by God to be the deliverer of God's People."

1. Locate Jerusalem, Jacobs Well, Cana and Capernaum on a map and then trace the route that Jesus and His disciples took to walk from Jerusalem to their home in Galilee. Is there anything interesting about the route?

2. Underline and highlight key words and phrases from John 4 and explain what you believe those are important.

3. Research the Samaritans. Who are they? What is their history with the people of Israel?

4. Research Jacob's well. Why is this location important to the people of Israel?

5. Think like a detective…

Make inferences and summarize why it might be significant that Jesus is talking to a "Samaritan woman" at Jacobs well.

Can we trust that the miracles of Jesus were real?

50 days after The Passover, where Jesus was crucified, the Jewish people gathered in Israel for another feast.

It was the feast of Pentecost, and it celebrated the giving of the law to Moses at Mount Sinai.

During the feast there were a few strange things that happened that year.

One of the things that happened out of the ordinary was a fisherman by the name of Peter, who is reported to have been a close friend and disciple of Jesus the Nazarene, preached a sermon.

During his sermon, Peter made this claim...

> *"People of Israel, listen! God publicly endorsed Jesus the Nazarene by doing powerful miracles, wonders, and signs through him, in your midst, as you well know."*

Peter, the Fisherman
Acts 2:22

THINK LIKE A DETECTIVE...

1. Do miracles prove that Jesus is the Messiah? Explain your position.

2. We know from the testimony of Acts 2 that there were more than 3,000 people gathered to hear Peter's sermon that morning. What is significant about his claim that the miracles were done in the presence of that many people?

Can we trust that the miracles of Jesus were real?

The fact that Jesus performed miracles was not a secret. The miracles, signs and wonders performed by Jesus happened in front of thousands of people. As one scholar notes, "The question was not, Did Jesus perform miracles?' What was in question was under what authority or power were the miracles accomplished. https://www.josh.org/christ-miracle-matters/

Fragments of both Christian and non-Christian testimony outside of the Bible about the miracles of Jesus Christ exist. Here are some samples of Christian sources.

Quadratus, a Greek church leader in Athens wrote a letter in the early 2nd century that stated...

"Our Savior's works, moreover, were always present: for they were real, consisting of those who had been healed of their diseases, those who had been raised from the dead; who were not only seen while they were being healed and raised up, but were afterwards constantly present.

Nor did they remain only during the sojourn of the Savior on earth, but also a considerable time after His departure; and, indeed, some of them have survived even down to our own times."

Josephus, a historian who was Jewish but not a follower of Christ write that Jesus was known as *"a worker of amazing deeds."*

The early church father Irenaeus wrote the following testimony about Polycarp. Polycarp was a known disciple of John the disciple of Jesus and would be burned at the stake for his faith.

"I can even describe the place where the blessed Polycarp used to sit and discourse— his going out, too, and his coming in—his general mode of life and personal appearance, together with the discourses which he delivered to the people; also how he would speak of his familiar intercourse with John, and with the rest of those who had seen the Lord; and how he would call their words to remembrance.

Whatsoever things he had heard from them respecting the Lord, both with regard to His miracles and His teaching, Polycarp having received from the eye-witnesses of the Word of life, would recount them all in harmony with the Scriptures."

Justin Martyr, who would be arrested in Rome for his faith in Christ as the miracle working Messiah wrote...

"And that it was predicted that our Christ should heal all diseases and raise the dead, hear what was said. There are these words: 'At His coming the lame shall leap like a deer, and the tongue of the stammerer shall be clear speaking: the blind shall see, and the lepers shall be cleansed; and the dead shall rise, and walk about.'

And that He did those things, you can learn from the Acts of Pontius Pilate." (Justin Martyr, First Apology, Chapter 48).

What makes the words of Justin significant?

Think like a Detective

Do miracles prove that Jesus is the Messiah?

The Jesus Film © 2003. https://arc.gt/yii25

What happened at Cana?

Genesis 1 opens with the words, "In the beginning" and then goes on to inform the reader how God created the world in 6 days.

John 1 opens with the words, "In the beginning," and then verse three informs the reader that all things were created by Jesus. In John 2, we see Jesus the bridegroom (Mark 2:19-20, Luke 5:34-35) attending a Wedding Feast in Cana.

This is highly symbolic in a Gospel where John declares his primary purpose is that we "believe that Jesus is the Christ."

In one of the other books authored by John, the book of Revelation, John ends the book with the prophecy that one day Jesus, the bridegroom, will return and celebrate the wedding feast between Himself and His bride.

The Miracle

In John 2, we read that Yeshua instantly changed the molecular structure of over 150 gallons of water contained in six separate jars cut from stone.

Each jar representing a single day of creation and the context of the wedding feast foretelling how

It was in one miracle that Jesus declared Himself both the Alpha and the Omega. The beginning and the end.

John was reminding his readers of creation and was declaring that Jesus has the power to create and was making a connection to the wedding feast at the end of time, reminding his readers that Jesus is our bridegroom.

In Cana of Galilee, Yeshua manifested His glory; and His disciples believed in Him.

John 2:11

#	Miracle	Matthew	Mark	Luke	John	Acts
1	Born of a virgin	1:18-25		1:26-28		
2	Water to wine				2:1-11	
3	Drives out an evil spirit in Capernaum		1:21-27	4:31-36		
4	Healing an Officials son in Capernaum				4:43-54	
5	Healing Peter's Mother in law in Capernaum	8:14-15	1:29-31	4:38-39		
6	Healing many in the evening	8:16-17	1:32-34	4:40-41		
7	Miraculous catch of fish on Lake Gennesaret			5:1-11		
8	Heals man with leprosy	8:1-4	1:40-45	5:12-14		
9	Heals Centurion's Servant in Capernaum	8:5-13		7:1-10		
10	Heals a paralyzed man who was let down through the roof	9:1-8	2:1-12	5:17-26		
11	Heals a mans withered hand on the Sabbath	12:9-14	3:1-6	6:6-11		
12	Raises a widow's son from the dead			7:11-17		
13	Calms a storm	8:23-27	4:35-41	8:22-25		
14	Casts demons into a herd of pigs	8:28-33	5:1-20	8:26-39		
15	Heals a woman with an issue of blood	9:20-22	5:25-34	8:42-48		
16	Raises Jairus' daughter back to life	9:18, 23-26	5:21-24, 35-43	8:40-42, 49-56		
17	Heals two blind men	9:27-31				
18	Heals a man unable to speak	9:32-34				
19	Heals an invalid in Bethesda				5:1-15	
20	Feeds 5,000	14:13-21	6:30-44	9:10-17	6:1-15	
21	Walks on the water	14:22-33	6:45-52		6:16-21	
22	Heals many sick people as they touch his garment	14:34-36	6:45-52			
23	Heals a Gentile woman's demon-possessed daughter	15:21-28	7:24-30			
24	Heals a man who is deaf and mute		7:31-37			
25	Feeds 4,000	15:32-39	8:1-13			
26	Heals a blind man at Bethsaida		8:22-26			
27	Heals a boy with an unclean spirit	17:14-20	9:14-29	9:37-43		
28	Heals a man born blind				9:1-38	
29	Produces the Temple tax from the fish's mouth	17:24-27				
30	Heals a blind and mute demon-possessed man	12:22-23		11:14-23		
31	Heals a woman who has been crippled for 18 years			13:10-17		
32	Heals a man on the Sabbath			14:1-6		
33	Heals 10 lepers			17:11-19		
34	Raises Lazarus from the dead				11:1-45	
35	Restores sight to Bartimaeus in Jericho	20:29-34	10:46-52	18:35-43		
36	Withers a fig tree	21:18:22	11:12-14			
37	Heals the servant's ear during his arrest			20:50-51		
38	Resurrection from the dead	28		24	20	
39	Miraculous catch of fish at the sea of Tiberias				21:4-11	
40	Ascended into heaven					1:1-11

Think like a Detective

Do miracles prove that Jesus is the Messiah?

Good Detectives decide if the witnesses are making statements are are facts or opinions.

How to write a summary

A summary is a shortened version of a longer reading that tells the basic ideas of the text or passage.

A summary should be

A. Short (3-5 sentences).
B. Focused on the main ideas.
C. Use both your words AND key words from the text.
D. Be focused on the description and not include opinion or personal feelings about the text.

Fact vs. Opinion

How do you <u>know</u> something is <u>true</u>? It is important to know the difference between a <u>fact</u> and an <u>opinion</u>.

- **A <u>fact</u> is a statement that can be proved or verified.**
- **<u>Facts</u> are certain and true.**
- **An <u>opinion</u> is a statement of personal belief or feeling.**
- **<u>Opinions</u> vary.**

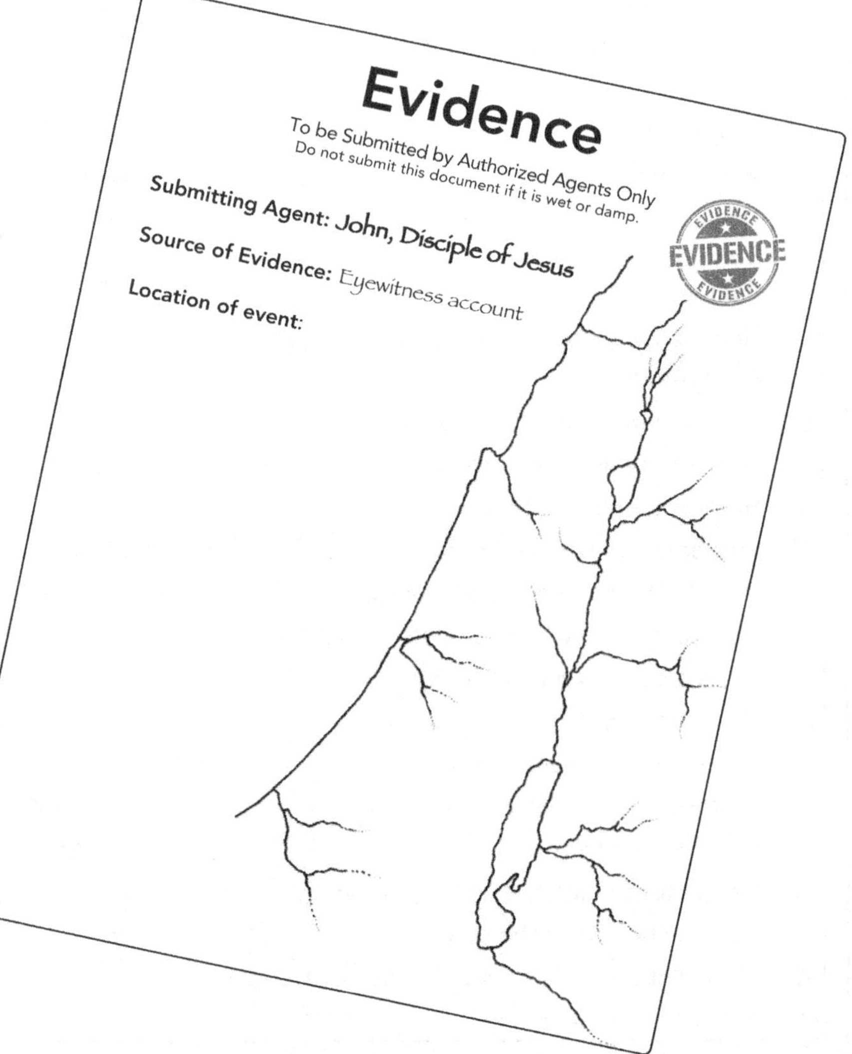

Does the life of Christ fulfill the lives of the Act I Patriarchs?

Is Yeshua a prophet like Moses?

As we continue to investigate the question of whether Jesus could have been the Messiah and if His life met the requirements of that God promised his people that the deliverer would meet, we need to examine if Yeshua was a prophet like Moses.

Twice in Deuteronomy 18, God promises that He will raise up a prophet that is "like Moses."

What does it mean to be a prophet "like Moses?"

> *"The Lord your God will raise up for you a prophet like me from among you, from your brothers – it is to him you shall listen".*
> *Deuteronomy 18:15*
>
> *"I will raise up for them a prophet like you from among their brothers. And I will put my words in his mouth, and he shall speak to them all that I command him. And whoever will not listen to my words that he shall speak in my name,*
> *I myself will require it of him."*
> *Deuteronomy 18:18*

Remember, in the Hebrew Scriptures that there were three major offices that God used to lead His people.

- The office of the **prophet**.
- The office of the **priest**.
- The office of the **King**.

The office of the **prophet** was to proclaim the word of God to His people. Prophets would receive God's word and then proclaim it with the authority of God's voice.

The office of the **priest** was to mediate between God and humans. For example, the priest would enter the Holy of Holies and offer sacrifices for the sins of the people.

The office of the king was to lead the people. The king would command the people, and they would obey him.

Moses fulfilled all three of these roles in ways that the leaders who followed him would not.

For example, Samuel acted as a prophet and priest, but he anointed Saul and David to be the king.

In the case of Jesus of Nazareth, one of the ways that He was a prophet like Moses is that He also would fulfill all three roles.

Think about it... How does Jesus fulfill the roles of prophet, priest, and king?

PATRIARCH

Is Yeshua the Messiah?

In this part of the investigation, you will be examining the testimony of the witnesses against the lives of the Old Testament Patriarchs to determine if the life of Christ reflects and fulfills the lives of the patriarchs.

You will examine;

- Yeshua and Adam
- Yeshua and Joseph
- Yeshua and Moses
- Yeshua and Joshua
- Yeshua and David

Yeshua is the one who delivers God's people. Like Joshua, who led the people out of the wilderness and into the Promised land, Jesus opens the door for us to leave the wilderness of sin and disobedience and follow Him into the land and the life that He has promised to those who love Him.

Yeshua (Joshua) meaning, "Yahweh, God is salvation" can also be translated as "one who delivers God's people."

Compare & Contrast

Hide & Seek?

In Genesis 3, the Lord God was in the garden of Eden seeking those who had hidden from Him because of their sin.

Luke records that when Jesus walked on the earth it was to seek and to save the lost.
Luke 19:10

How does the life of Moses reflect the life of Christ?

MOSES	YESHUA
Moses is born a Hebrew Jew from the tribe of Levi	Yeshua is born a Jew from the tribe of Judah
Moses was a shepherd	Jesus claims to be the good shepherd.
Arrives on the scene after 400 years of what seems to be inactivity of God.	Arrives on the scene after 400 years of what seems to be inactivity of God.
Fasted for 40 Days on Mount Sinai	Fasted for 40 Days in the Wilderness
"Hidden" in Egypt during a proclamation by Pharaoh to kill all of the Hebrew babies.	"Hidden" in Egypt during a proclamation by Herod to kill all of the Hebrew babies.
Performed miracles to demonstrate that his authority was given by God.	Performed miracles to demonstrate that His authority was given by God.
Moses instituted the Passover and instructed the people regarding the Passover lamb.	Jesus celebrated the Passover and was the perfect and final Passover Lamb.
God audibly confirms His pleasure with Moses at Sinai.	God audibly confirms His pleasure with Yeshua at His baptism.
Moses left the palace and the riches of the Pharaoh to live a humble life of service.	Yeshua left the palace and the riches of the Kingdom of Heaven to live a life of service.
Moses served with humility (Numbers 12:3)	Christ served with humility (Philippians 2:5-8)
The life of Moses was preserved by Miriam (his sister).	The life of Yeshua was preserved by Miriam (his mother).
Mocked by his siblings (Numbers 12:1)	Mocked by His siblings (Mark 3:20-21).
Manna was sent from heaven to feed the people of God.	Jesus fed the multitude with a few small loaves.
50 days after the deliverance from their bondage in Egypt the people of Israel receive the law of God at Mount Sinai celebrating the first Pentecost.	50 days after the deliverance from sin through the death and resurrection of Christ, the people of God receive the Holy Spirit during the celebration of Pentecost.
Moses sends 12 spies to explore The Promised Land.	Yeshua sends 12 Disciples to proclaim the good news.
Moses appoints 70 rulers to lead Israel.	Yeshua sends out 70 disciples to proclaim the good news.
Moses is born and put into a basket (translated as Ark).	Yeshua is born and put into a basket (translated as manger).

How does the life of Adam reflect the life of Christ?

ADAM	YESHUA
Tempted by the words, "Did God really say?" Genesis 3:1	When Tempted He responded, "It is written." Matthew 4:4, 7,10
They ate from the tree in disobedience to God. Genesis 3:6	Hung on a tree in obedience to God.
Ate from the tree and realized they were naked.	Hung naked on the tree after having his clothing taken from Him.
Ate from the tree and felt fear when God approached.	Hung on the tree and cried out to God, "Why have you forsaken me."
Hid from God (3:10)	Claimed to come seeking and saving the lost
Blamed God and Eve for his sin (3:12)	Forgave those who hammered the nails.
God foretold that the offspring of Eve would have his heel bruised by the serpent (3:15).	Having His feet nailed to the cross would have caused bruising on the bottom heel as He used that foot to gain leverage and breath.
God foretold that the offspring of Eve would crush the head of the serpent (3:15).	Jesus breathed His last and said, "It is finished."
Told that the ground would now produce thorns (3:18).	Wore a crown of thorns.
Told that He would work and it would cause sweat on his brow (19).	Sweat drops of blood in anticipation of the cross and would bleed again from the crown of thorns.
Told he would return to the ground (3:19)	Was buried in a borrowed tomb.
Told that he would return to dust where he came from (3:19).	Rose from the dead. Returned to heaven where He came from.
God sacrificed an animal to cover their sin and shame (3:21).	Offered His life as our perfect sacrifice to cover our sin and shame.
Removed from the Garden and not allowed to touch the tree of life (22).	Removed from the Garden of Gethsemane and hung on the tree in order that we might have life.

Think like a Detective

How does the life of Isaac reflect the life of Christ?

ISAAC	YESHUA
Sacrifice as an act of obedience	Sacrifice as an act of obedience
The only son of Abraham	The only Son of God
Rides a donkey to Mount Moriah	Rides a donkey into Jerusalem (Mount Moriah)
Carries the wood for the sacrifice to the top of the mountain	Carries the wood for the sacrifice to the top of the mountain
God provides a ram who is caught among thorns.	Jesus is crowned with thorns as they are preparing Him for the cross.
Willingly goes to the altar and does not resist.	Willingly goes to the cross and does not resist.
Takes place on Mount Moriah	Takes place in the hills of Mount Moriah on Calvary.
God provides the sacrifice.	Jesus is the sacrifice who is provided by God.
Removed from the Garden and not allowed to touch the tree of life (22).	Removed from the Garden of Gethsemane and hung on the tree in order that we might have life.

Think like a Detective

How does the life of Joseph reflect the life of Christ?

JOSEPH	YESHUA
Betrayed by his brothers	Hated by his brothers
Resisted Temptation	Resisted Temptation
Forgave those who betrayed him	Forgave those who betrayed him
Accused between two criminals	Crucified between two criminals
One was destined for life and one for death	One was destined for life and one for death
Falsely accused	Falsely Accused
Falsely imprisoned	Falsely sent to the cross
Joseph asked the servant who was to be reinstated to remember him once he was back in Pharaoh's palace, but the scriptures tell us that the servant forgot about Joseph.	the man on Yeshua's right asked the Lord to remember him when he comes into His kingdom, and Yeshua told him that day he would be in Paradise with him – it was remembered and immediate.
3 days later their fate would be decided	3 days later He rose from the dead.
The two servants in prison with Joseph present the bread and wine to Joseph by virtue of their dreams. Remember we are told one had a dream about the grapes on the vine and how he pressed the juice into the cup. The other servant was a baker and in his dream was the bread in the basket.	Yeshua presented the bread and the wine to his disciples and the world. The bread is his body broken for us while the wine is his blood of the new covenant.
Redemption and forgiveness came in connection with the cup	Redemption and forgiveness cam in connection with the cup

Notes

Think like a Detective

How does the office of Levitical Priest reflect the life of Christ?

LEVITICAL PRIESTS	YESHUA
Many Priests	Jesus is the priest (Hebrews 7:23-24)
Priests were temporary	Jesus is the eternal priest (Hebrews 9:12)
Priests needed to make daily and repetitive sacrifices	Single sacrifice for all people at all times (Hebrews 7:27, 9:12)
The priests were sinful	Holy (Hebrews 7:26-27)
Priests needed to offer sacrifices for their won sin	Only offered sacrifices for the sins of others (Hebrews 7:26-27)
Priests sacrificed animals as a substitution	He was the priest and the sacrifice (Hebrews 7:27;9:11-14)
Priests entered into a tabernacle made by human hands	He entered into the perfect tent (Hebrews 9:11-12)
Priest she the blood of animals as their means for entrance	His own shed blood was the means for entrance (Hebrews 9:11-12).

Notes

Does Jesus claim to be God?

The name of God in the Hebrew Scriptures is a mystery. People often pronounce the four Hebrew letters (YHWH) as "Yahweh" or "Jehovah," but the truth is that we don't know how to say it. We don't even know how to pronounce it.

"Moses said to God, "Suppose I go to the sons of Israel and say to them, 'The God of your fathers has sent me to you,' and they ask me, 'What is His Name?' What should I say to them?"

"God answered Moses, **"I AM WHO I AM."**

Then He said, "You are to say to the sons of Israel, **'I AM'** has sent me to you."

God also said to Moses: "You are to say to the sons of Israel, Adonai (YHWH) **the God of your fathers, the God of Abraham, Isaac and Jacob**, has sent me to you.

This is My Name forever, and the Name by which I should be remembered from generation to generation."

Exodus 3:13-15

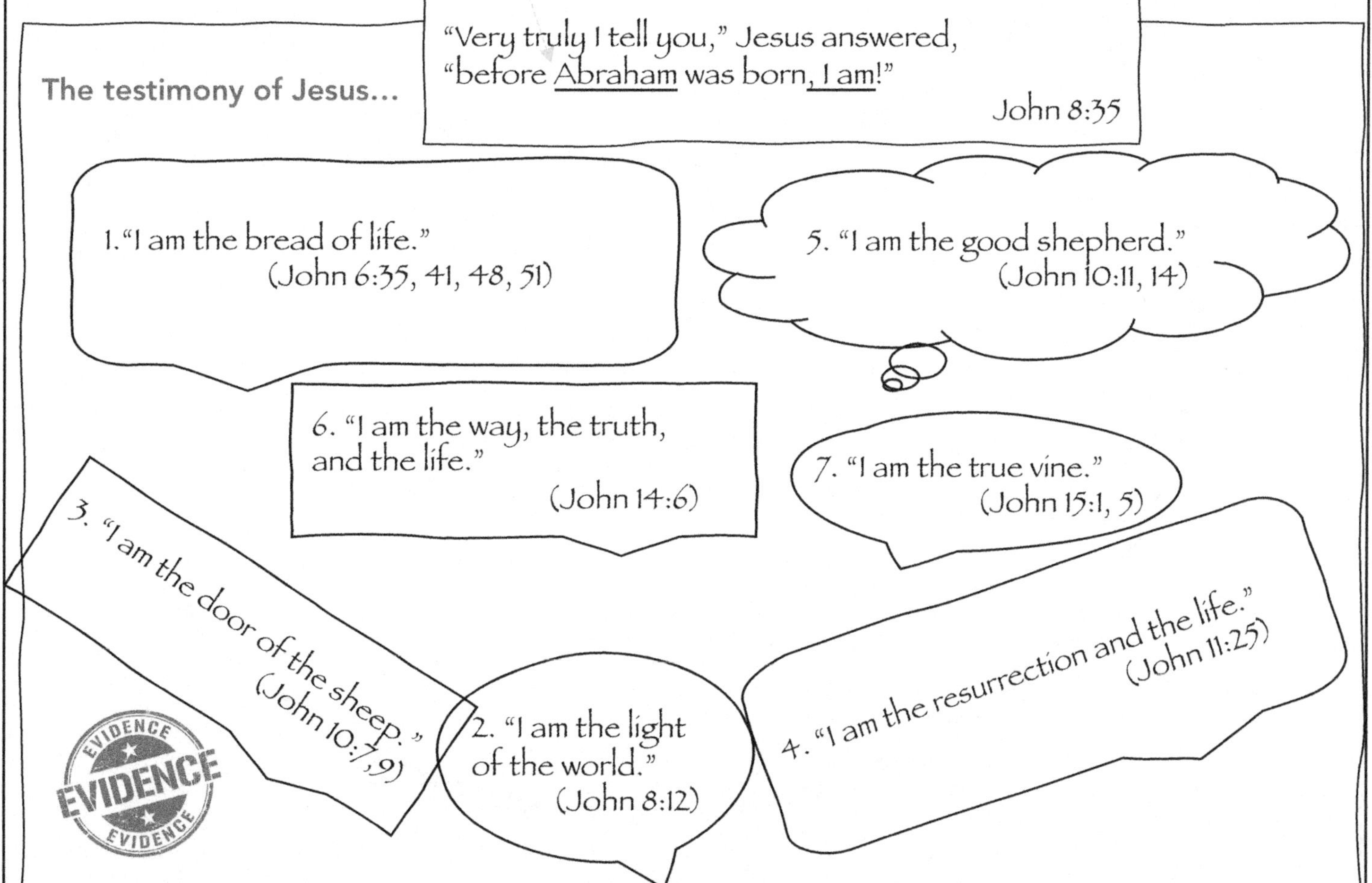

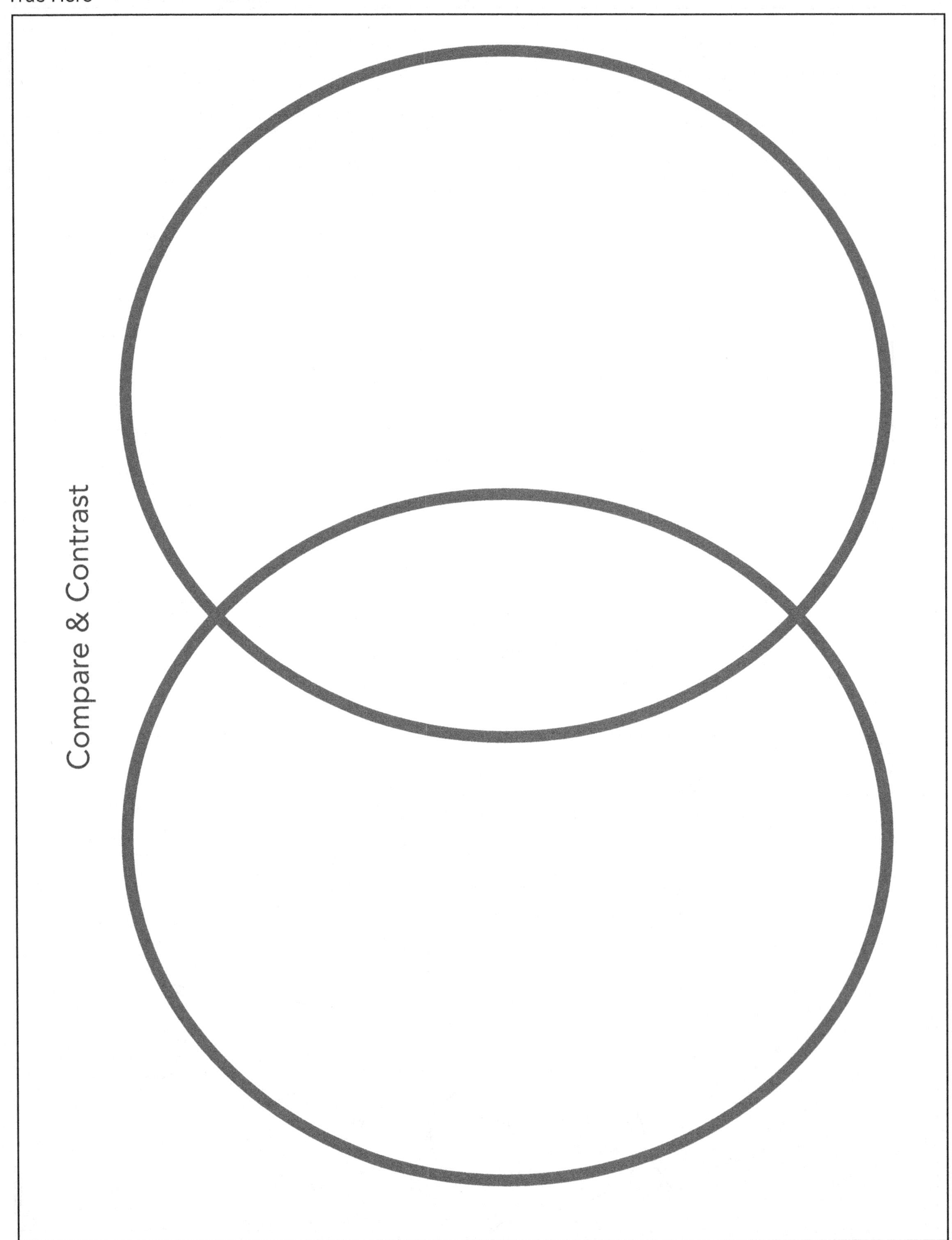
Compare & Contrast

Does the life of Christ fulfill the lives of the Act I Patriarchs?

Investigation Summary

Does the plot of the life of Jesus the Nazarene fulfill the threads of Scripture?

The Purple Thread

The Scarlet Thread

The Golden Thread

The Scarlet Thread

The Purple Thread

The Golden Thread

Evaluate like a Detective

The evidence board

Is Paul's claim correct? Does Jesus meet the requirements to be the Messiah?

1. Collect evidence.
2. Read like a detective.
3. Preserve the evidence.
4. **Evaluate the evidence.**
5. Cite the evidence.

Evidence Board

Inferences

Authors may hint at an idea without stating it directly.

You must use what you already know about a topic to make a connection and figure out what is being communicated.

- You make an inference by combining text clues with your background knowledge to arrive at a logical conclusion or an "educated guess."

Investigation Summary

To be Submitted by Authorized Agents Only
Do not submit this document if it is wet or damp.

EVIDENCE

Source of Evidence: ______________________________

Summary Description of Evidence:

____

____

____

____

____

____

____

____

____

____

____

____

____

____

____

____

____

Mission Report

EVIDENCE

CLASSIFIED

Detective Evaluation

COLLABORATION RUBRIC				
Notes and Plans: 				
	Below Standard	Approaching Standard	At Standard	Above Standard
Takes Personal Responsibility for Learning and Contributing to the Learning Process	• Is not prepared, informed or ready to contribute to the team • Does not utilize technology as agreed upon • Does not participate in project tasks • Does not listen to or use feedback to improve work	• Usually prepared, informed and ready to work with team • Does not utilize technology according to agreed upon standards with consistency • Needs reminding or prompting to complete tasks • Uses some feedback and complete most tasks	• Prepared and ready to work • Well informed and cites evidence that encourages learning among other team members • Consistently uses technology as agree upon • Self motivated and does not need to be reminded to complete tasks • Completes tasks on time • Evaluates and uses feedback to improve work	
Contribution to the Team	• Does not help the team to solve problems; may be the source of problems for the team • Does not ask probing questions, express ideas, or elaborate in response to questions or discussions • Do not offer help • Does not provide useful feedback	• Cooperates but does not actively participate in problem solving • Occasionally asks probing questions, expresses ideas, or elaborates in responses or discussions • Sometimes offers help • Sometimes provides feedback but it may not always be helpful	• Helps the team to solve problems and manage conflict • Clearly expresses ideas, asks probing questions, listens to others and solicits feedback from quiet team members to ensure that all perspectives are shared and heard • Provides useful feedback • Identifies opportunities to help others where appropriate	
Relationships and Respect	• Impolite or unkind to team members (may interrupt, ignore, talk over or use hurtful words or body language) • Does not listen or respect other perspectives	• Usually polite and kind to team members • Usually listens and respects team members • Disagrees with content, perspectives and opinions without attacking the person	• Polite and kind to team members • Listens to, acknowledges and respects other team members • Disagrees with content and builds community by affirming the person	

TRUE HERO

"The true story of the extraordinary mission of God"

passover

Learning to love God's Word

When they hurled their insults at him, he did not retaliate; when he suffered, he made no threats. Instead, he entrusted himself to him who judges justly. "He himself bore our sins" in his body on the cross, so that we might die to sins and live for righteousness; "by his wounds you have been healed."

1 Peter 2:23-24

But God demonstrates His love to us like this; while we were still sinners Christ died for us.

Romans 5:8

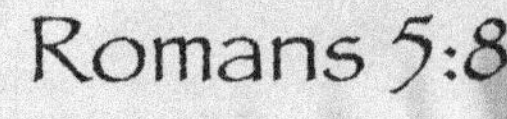

Did Jesus rise from the dead?

One of the keys to Paul's legal defense in front of Festus is the claim that Jesus of Nazareth was the Messiah and that He rose from the dead.

In the previous section of our investigation, we examined the question of whether or not Jesus was capable of miraculous or supernatural actions.

We even examined the idea that there were a few people who Jesus brought back to life after they had passed away, but is it possible that the story of His resurrection is also true?

The question for this part of our investigation is did Jesus of Nazareth rise from the dead?

Trial Testimony

I teach nothing except what the prophets and Moses said would happen– 23 that the Messiah would suffer and be the first to rise from the dead, and in this way, announce God's light to Jews and Gentiles alike."

Suddenly, Festus shouted, "Paul, you are insane. Too much study has made you crazy!"

But Paul replied, "I am not insane, Most Excellent Festus. What I am saying is the sober truth.

And King Agrippa knows about these things. I speak boldly, for I am sure these events are all familiar to him, for they were not done in a corner!

Acts 26:23-26

Making the connection

What is the connection between the two gardens

In the beginning of the book of Genesis, God gives Adam the mission to reflect the glory of God and to fill the earth with that glory.

But sadly, Adam chooses to rebel against the will of God and to chase after his own glory.

The Bible refers to Jesus Christ as the "second Adam" because, like Adam, Jesus is born without the taint of sin.

On the night before His crucifixion, when Jesus enters into the Garden of Gethsemane to pray , He is given the same choice as Adam. He can obey the will of the Father and bring glory to His name in heaven and on earth; or He can do His own will.

The Garden of Gethsemane

39 And He came out and proceeded as was
His custom to the Mount of Olives; and the
disciples also followed Him. 40 When He
arrived at the place, He said to them, "Pray
that you may not enter into temptation."
41 And He withdrew from them about a stone's
throw, and He knelt down and began to pray,
42 saying, "Father, if You are willing, remove
this cup from Me; yet not My will, but Yours be
done." 43 Now an angel from heaven
appeared to Him, strengthening Him. 44 And
being in agony He was praying very fervently;
and His sweat became like drops of blood,
falling down upon the ground.

Luke 22:39-44

"Not my will but yours be done." Jesus

Does the resurrection matter?

Why is the resurrection so important?

Because without it, the Christian faith has no foundation. In his letter to the church in Corinth, Paul states the centrality of the resurrection like this...

"If Jesus has not been raised, then our faith is worthless; and we are to be pitied above all men."

1Corinthians 15

Explain Paul's statement in your own words.

Do you agree with him?

Why or why not?

CRIME SCENE DO NOT CROSS

Did Jesus really rise from the dead?

Alternate theories of the resurrection

During this unit, you will be investigating the resurrection of Jesus Christ.

In the first units, you examined whether the eyewitnesses were reliable and credible.

In this unit, you will be relying on the eyewitness accounts as well as secondhand accounts from non-biblical witnesses.

As Paul makes his defense before King Agrippa, he not only makes the claim that Jesus of Nazareth rose from the dead but that the events were "not done in a corner."

Yet over the years, there have been many different alternative theories to what happened to Jesus after he was crucified.

Many different people have tried to explain away the idea that Jesus claimed to be God and that He rose from the dead.

For followers of Christ, like Paul, it is foundational to be able to trust that it is reasonable to believe that Jesus rose from the dead and that the alternative theories are false.

In this unit, you will need to think like a detective and;

1. Identify alternative theories.
2. Identify clues from the eyewitnesses.
3. Closely read the eyewitness testimony.
4. Discuss what you uncover with your team of detectives.
5. Decide what you think is the best explanation of the evidence.

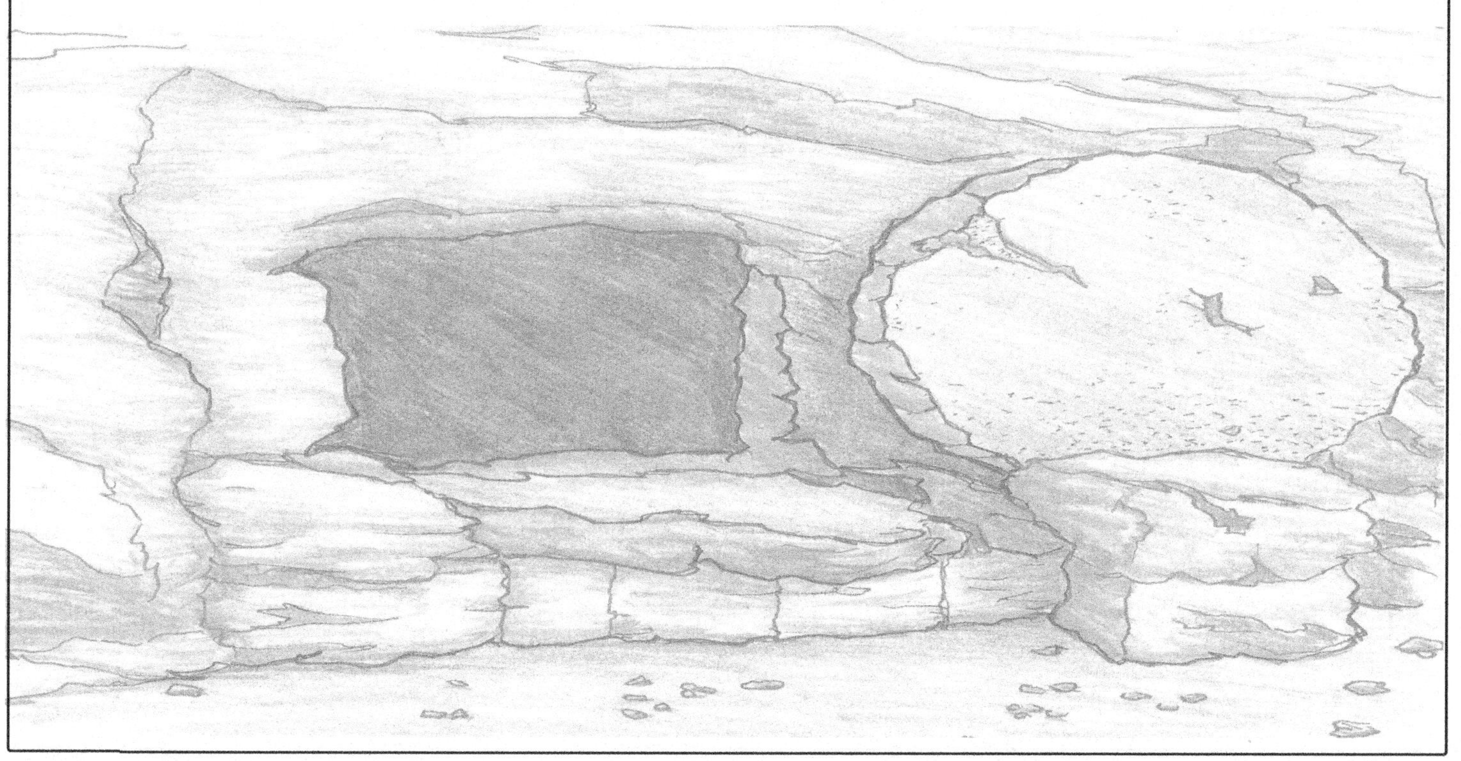

Alternate Theories on the Resurrection

Investigate the evidence

Think like a detective

1. Sort the evidence.
2. Identify your conclusions.
3. State your position.

Unknown Tomb Theory

Existential Resurrection Theory

Legend Theory

Spiritual Resurrection Theory

CRIME SCENE

Wrong Tomb Theory

Hallucination Theory

The Passover Plot Theory

The Swoon Theory (Resuscitation)

Stolen Body Theory

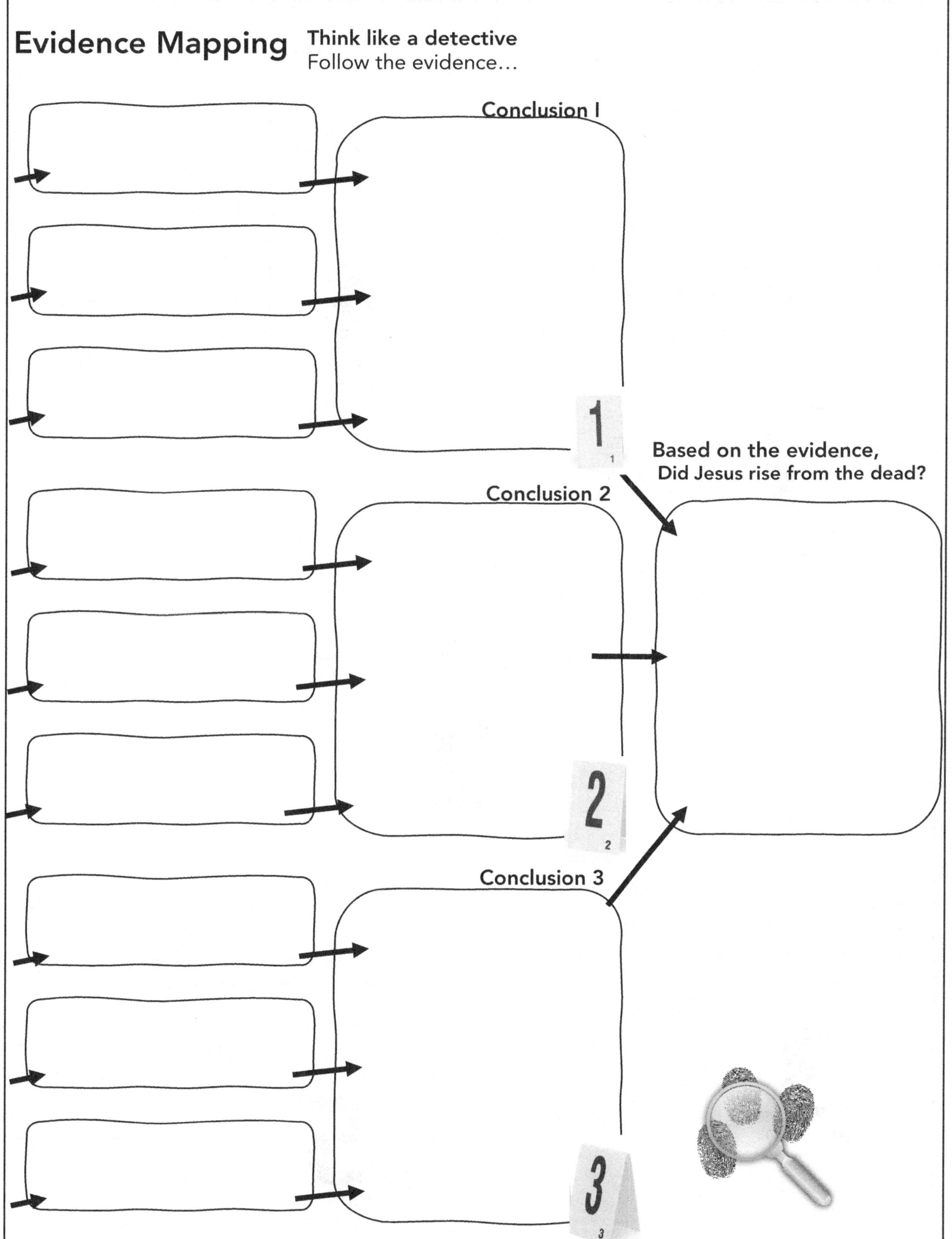
Evidence Mapping
Think like a detective
Follow the evidence…
Conclusion 1
1
Conclusion 2
Based on the evidence,
Did Jesus rise from the dead?
2
Conclusion 3
3

Did Jesus really rise from the dead?
Alternate theories of the resurrection
Joseph of Arimathea who was a member of the Jewish Council requested permission from the Roman Governor Pilate to bury Jesus in his family tomb. There were eyewitnesses to where Christ was buried.
1
EVIDENCE
TRUE HERO
Notes:
The women watched the body being prepared for burial and knew the location.
4
EVIDENCE
TRUE HERO
Notes:
Paul wrote to the Church in Corinth (AD 55) appealing to the fact that over 500 eyewitnesses, who had seen Jesus in various places and at various times, existed, many of whom were still alive and available to confirm that they had seen Christ resurrected.
2
EVIDENCE
TRUE HERO
Notes:
The women arrived at the tomb expecting it to be sealed.
3
EVIDENCE
TRUE HERO
Notes:
Christ ate food. He touched people. He made a fire. He picked up fish.
5
EVIDENCE
TRUE HERO
Notes:

The Romans stationed guards at the tomb because the Jews feared that someone may try to take the body.
6
EVIDENCE
TRUE HERO
Notes:
The Romans had soldiers guarding the tomb. Failure to guard the body would have resulted in death.
7
EVIDENCE
TRUE HERO
Notes:
The man they met is quoted as saying, "He is not here. He is risen."
8
EVIDENCE
TRUE HERO
Notes:
The Jews, Romans, Joseph of Arimathea all knew the location of the tomb and could easily have identified it.
9
EVIDENCE
TRUE HERO
Notes:
At any point, Jewish leaders could have proven that Christ was still dead by showing people the occupied tomb. They never did.
10
EVIDENCE
TRUE HERO
Notes:
The disciples would have known Jesus after living with him for nearly three years. Their change from men who fled at his arrest to men who gave their lives because they believed He rose from the dead is too dramatic to be based on a trick.
11
EVIDENCE
TRUE HERO
Notes:

Medical science demonstrates that Christ could not have survived the process of being whipped, nailed to the cross, stabbed in the side and the overall loss of blood.
12
EVIDENCE
TRUE HERO
Notes:
The disciples (and over 500 eyewitnesses) were utterly convinced that the physical resurrection of Christ was a real event.
13
EVIDENCE
TRUE HERO
Notes:
There is zero evidence from His childhood or anyone who knew Him that Jesus had a twin (including the testimony of His brothers who despised Him).
14
EVIDENCE
TRUE HERO
Notes:
How could a nearly dead man, without medical attention make such a dramatic impression on people that He was not only risen from the dead but at full health?
15
EVIDENCE
TRUE HERO
Notes:
Sleeping on duty would have resulted in death for the Roman soldiers.
16
EVIDENCE
TRUE HERO
Notes:
The disciples were not expecting Christ to rise from the dead.
17
EVIDENCE
TRUE HERO
Notes:

The same disciples who fled at His arrest gave their lives for the belief that He rose from the dead. How could they have mustered the courage to attack Roman Soldiers and then died for a story they knew was a lie
18
EVIDENCE
TRUE HERO
Notes:
Fishermen untrained in swordsmanship (ie: Peter) could never have overpowered a group of Roman soldiers.
19
EVIDENCE
TRUE HERO
Notes:
Jesus interacted with people in groups and not just individually. Hallucinations are typically not "shared" events. They occur with individuals.
20
EVIDENCE
TRUE HERO
Notes:

The Trial of Jesus of Nazareth

Matthew 27:11-23

11 Meanwhile Jesus stood before the
governor, and the governor asked him, "Are
you the king of the Jews?"

"You have said so," Jesus replied.

12 When he was accused by the chief priests
and the elders, he gave no answer.13 Then
Pilate asked him, "Don't you hear the
testimony they are bringing against
you?" 14 But Jesus made no reply, not even to
a single charge—to the great amazement of
the governor.

15 Now it was the governor's custom at the
festival to release a prisoner chosen by the
crowd. 16 At that time they had a well-known
prisoner whose name was Jesus
Barabbas. 17 So when the crowd had
gathered, Pilate asked them, "Which one do
you want me to release to you: Jesus Barabbas,
or Jesus who is called the Messiah?"

18 For he knew it was out of self-interest that
they had handed Jesus over to him.

19 While Pilate was sitting on the judge's
seat, his wife sent him this message: "Don't
have anything to do with that innocent man, for
I have suffered a great deal today in a
dream because of him."

20 But the chief priests and the elders
persuaded the crowd to ask for Barabbas and
to have Jesus executed.

21 "Which of the two do you want me to
release to you?" asked the governor.

"Barabbas," they answered.

22 "What shall I do, then, with Jesus who is
called the Messiah?" Pilate asked.

They all answered, "Crucify him!"

23 "Why? What crime has he committed?"
asked Pilate.

But they shouted all the louder, "Crucify him!"

The Trial of Jesus of Nazareth

Matthew 27:24-40

24 When Pilate saw that he was getting
nowhere, but that instead an uproar was
starting, he took water and washed his hands in
front of the crowd. "I am innocent of this man's
blood," he said. "It is your responsibility!"

25 All the people answered, "His blood is on us
and on our children!"

26 Then he released Barabbas to them. But he
had Jesus flogged, and handed him over to be
crucified.

27 Then the governor's soldiers took Jesus into
the Praetorium and gathered the whole
company of soldiers around him. 28 They
stripped him and put a scarlet robe on
him, 29 and then twisted together a crown of
thorns and set it on his head. They put a staff in
his right hand.

Then they knelt in front of him and mocked
him. "Hail, king of the Jews!" they said. 30 They
spit on him and took the staff and struck him
on the head again and again. 31 After they had
mocked him, they took off the robe and put his
own clothes on him. Then they led him away to
crucify him.

32 As they were going out, they met a man from
Cyrene, named Simon, and they forced him to
carry the cross. 33 They came to a place called
Golgotha (which means "the place of the
skull"). 34 There they offered Jesus wine to
drink, mixed with gall; but after tasting it, he
refused to drink it. 35 When they had crucified
him, they divided up his clothes by casting
lots. 36 And sitting down, they kept watch over
him there. 37 Above his head they placed the
written charge against him: this is Jesus, the
King of the Jews.

38 Two rebels were crucified with him, one on
his right and one on his left. 39 Those who
passed by hurled insults at him, shaking their
heads 40 and saying, "You who are going to
destroy the temple and build it in three
days, save yourself! Come down from the cross,
if you are the Son of God!"

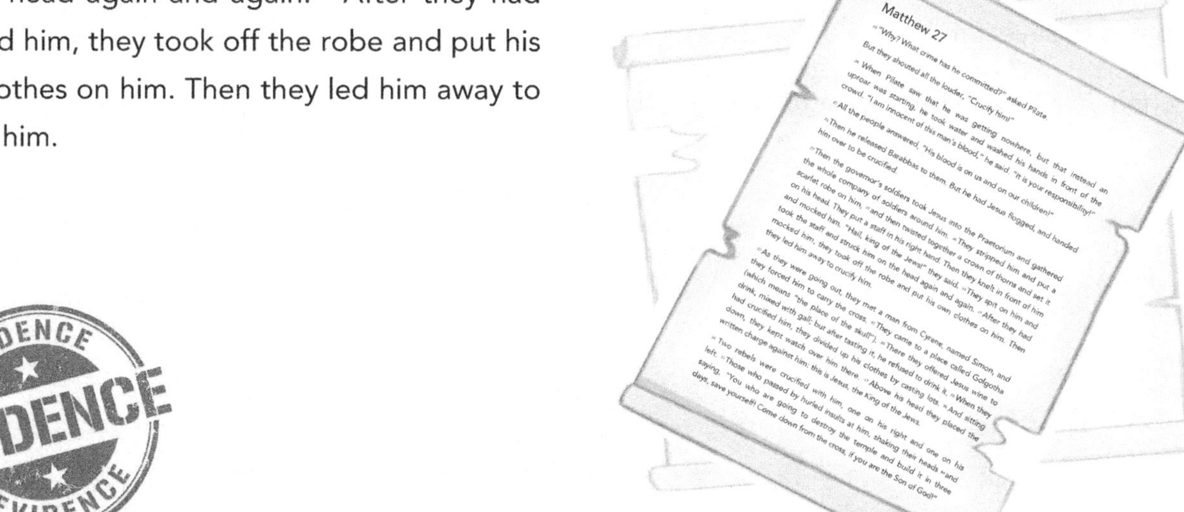

The Trial of Jesus of Nazareth

Matthew 27:41-56

41 In the same way the chief priests, the teachers
of the law and the elders mocked him. 42 "He
saved others," they said, "but he can't save
himself! He's the king of Israel! Let him come
down now from the cross, and we will
believe in him. 43 He trusts in God. Let God
rescue him now if he wants him, for he said, 'I
am the Son of God.'" 44 In the same way the
rebels who were crucified with him also heaped
insults on him.

45 From noon until three in the afternoon
darkness came over all the land. 46 About three
in the afternoon Jesus cried out in a loud
voice, "Eli, Eli lema sabachthani?" (which
means "My God, my God, why have you
forsaken me?").

47 When some of those standing there heard
this, they said, "He's calling Elijah."

48 Immediately one of them ran and got a
sponge. He filled it with wine vinegar, put it on
a staff, and offered it to Jesus to drink. 49 The
rest said, "Now leave him alone. Let's see if
Elijah comes to save him."

50 And when Jesus had cried out again in a loud
voice, he gave up his spirit.

51 At that moment the curtain of the
temple was torn in two from top to bottom.
The earth shook, the rocks split 52 and the
tombs broke open. The bodies of many holy
people who had died were raised to
life. 53 They came out of the tombs after
Jesus' resurrection and went into the holy
city and appeared to many people.

54 When the centurion and those with him who
were guarding Jesus saw the earthquake and
all that had happened, they were terrified,
and exclaimed, "Surely he was the Son of
God!"

55 Many women were there, watching from a
distance. They had followed Jesus from
Galilee to care for his needs. 56 Among them
were Mary Magdalene, Mary the mother of
James and Joseph, and the mother of
Zebedee's sons.

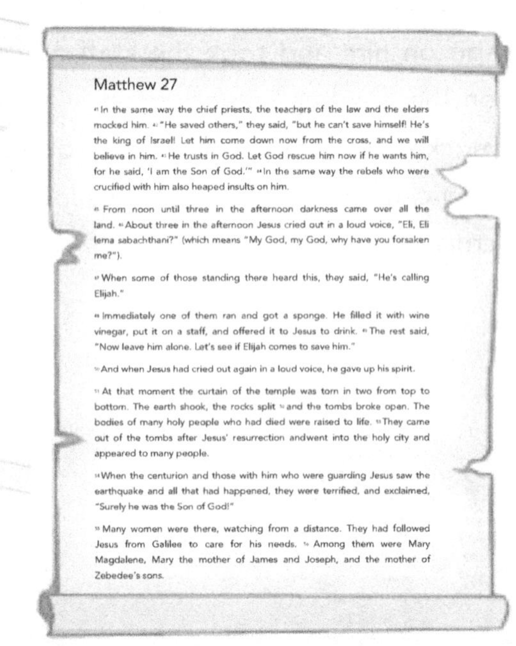

Matthew 27

41 In the same way the chief priests, the teachers of the law and the elders
mocked him. 42 "He saved others," they said, "but he can't save himself! He's
the king of Israel! Let him come down now from the cross, and we will
believe in him. 43 He trusts in God. Let God rescue him now if he wants him,
for he said, 'I am the Son of God.'" 44 In the same way the rebels who were
crucified with him also heaped insults on him.

45 From noon until three in the afternoon darkness came over all the
land. 46 About three in the afternoon Jesus cried out in a loud voice, "Eli, Eli
lema sabachthani?" (which means "My God, my God, why have you forsaken
me?").

47 When some of those standing there heard this, they said, "He's calling
Elijah."

48 Immediately one of them ran and got a sponge. He filled it with wine
vinegar, put it on a staff, and offered it to Jesus to drink. 49 The rest said,
"Now leave him alone. Let's see if Elijah comes to save him."

50 And when Jesus had cried out again in a loud voice, he gave up his spirit.

51 At that moment the curtain of the temple was torn in two from top to
bottom. The earth shook, the rocks split 52 and the tombs broke open. The
bodies of many holy people who had died were raised to life. 53 They came
out of the tombs after Jesus' resurrection andwent into the holy city and
appeared to many people.

54 When the centurion and those with him who were guarding Jesus saw the
earthquake and all that had happened, they were terrified, and exclaimed,
"Surely he was the Son of God!"

55 Many women were there, watching from a distance. They had followed
Jesus from Galilee to care for his needs. 56 Among them were Mary
Magdalene, Mary the mother of James and Joseph, and the mother of
Zebedee's sons.

The Trial of Jesus of Nazareth

Matthew 27:57-66

57 As evening approached, there came a rich
man from Arimathea, named Joseph, who had
himself become a disciple of Jesus. 58 Going to
Pilate, he asked for Jesus' body, and Pilate
ordered that it be given to him. 59 Joseph took
the body, wrapped it in a clean linen
cloth, 60 and placed it in his own new tomb that
he had cut out of the rock. He rolled a big
stone in front of the entrance to the tomb and
went away. 61 Mary Magdalene and the other
Mary were sitting there opposite the tomb.

62 The next day, the one after Preparation Day,
the chief priests and the Pharisees went to
Pilate. 63 "Sir," they said, "we remember that
while he was still alive that deceiver said, 'After
three days I will rise again.' 64 So give the order
for the tomb to be made secure until the third
day. Otherwise, his disciples may come and
steal the body and tell the people that he has
been raised from the dead. This last deception
will be worse than the first."

65 "Take a guard," Pilate answered. "Go, make
the tomb as secure as you know how." 66 So
they went and made the tomb secure by
putting a seal on the stone and posting the
guard.

Matthew 28:1-4

After the Sabbath, at dawn on the first day of
the week, Mary Magdalene and the other
Mary went to look at the tomb.

2 There was a violent earthquake, for an
angel of the Lord came down from heaven and,
going to the tomb, rolled back the stone and
sat on it. 3 His appearance was like lightning,
and his clothes were white as snow. 4 The
guards were so afraid of him that they shook
and became like dead men.

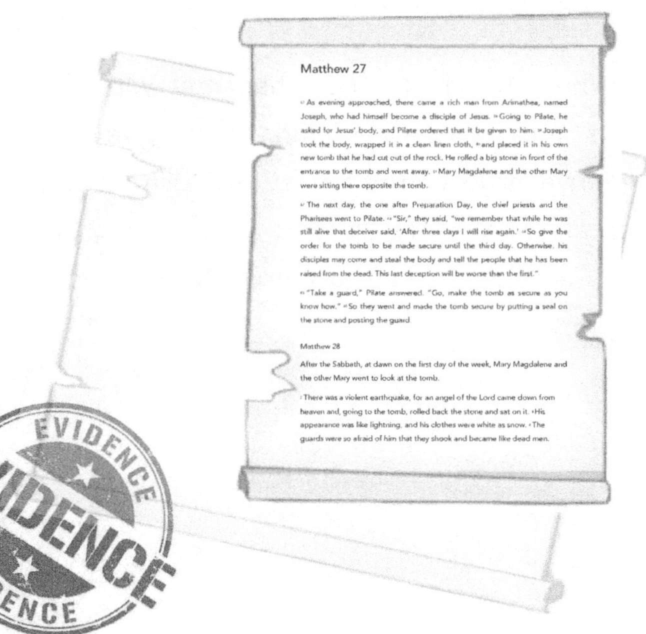
Matthew 27

57 As evening approached, there came a rich man from Arimathea, named Joseph, who had himself become a disciple of Jesus. 58 Going to Pilate, he asked for Jesus' body, and Pilate ordered that it be given to him. 59 Joseph took the body, wrapped it in a clean linen cloth, 60 and placed it in his own new tomb that he had cut out of the rock. He rolled a big stone in front of the entrance to the tomb and went away. 61 Mary Magdalene and the other Mary were sitting there opposite the tomb.

62 The next day, the one after Preparation Day, the chief priests and the Pharisees went to Pilate. 63 "Sir," they said, "we remember that while he was still alive that deceiver said, 'After three days I will rise again.' 64 So give the order for the tomb to be made secure until the third day. Otherwise, his disciples may come and steal the body and tell the people that he has been raised from the dead. This last deception will be worse than the first."

65 "Take a guard," Pilate answered. "Go, make the tomb as secure as you know how." 66 So they went and made the tomb secure by putting a seal on the stone and posting the guard.

Matthew 28

After the Sabbath, at dawn on the first day of the week, Mary Magdalene and the other Mary went to look at the tomb.

2 There was a violent earthquake, for an angel of the Lord came down from heaven and, going to the tomb, rolled back the stone and sat on it. 3 His appearance was like lightning, and his clothes were white as snow. 4 The guards were so afraid of him that they shook and became like dead men.

The Trial of Jesus of Nazareth

Matthew 28:5-20

5 The angel said to the women, "Do not be
afraid, for I know that you are looking for Jesus,
who was crucified. 6 He is not here; he has
risen, just as he said. Come and see the place
where he lay. 7 Then go quickly and tell his
disciples: 'He has risen from the dead and is
going ahead of you into Galilee. There you will
see him.' Now I have told you."

8 So the women hurried away from the tomb,
afraid yet filled with joy, and ran to tell his
disciples. 9 Suddenly Jesus met
them. "Greetings," he said. They came to him,
clasped his feet and worshiped him. 10 Then
Jesus said to them, "Do not be afraid. Go and
tell my brothers to go to Galilee; there they will
see me."

11 While the women were on their way, some
of the guards went into the city and reported
to the chief priests everything that had
happened.

12 When the chief priests had met with the
elders and devised a plan, they gave the
soldiers a large sum of money, 13 telling them,
"You are to say, 'His disciples came during the
night and stole him away while we were
asleep.'

14 If this report gets to the governor, we will
satisfy him and keep you out of trouble." 15 So
the soldiers took the money and did as they
were instructed. And this story has been widely
circulated among the Jews to this very day.

16 Then the eleven disciples went to Galilee, to
the mountain where Jesus had told them to
go. 17 When they saw him, they worshiped
him; but some doubted.18 Then Jesus came to
them and said, "All authority in heaven and on
earth has been given to me.

19 Therefore go and make disciples of all
nations, baptizing them in the name of the
Father and of the Son and of the Holy
Spirit, 20 and teaching them to obey
everything I have commanded you. And surely,
I am with you always, to the very end of the
age."

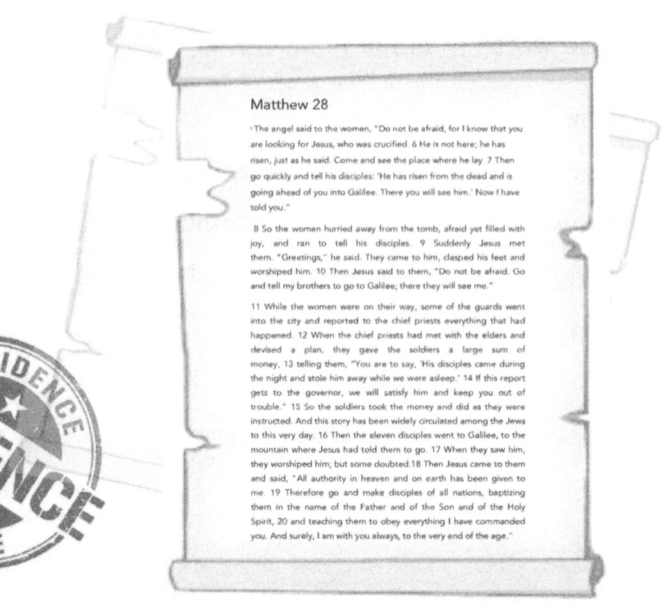

Matthew 28

5 The angel said to the women, "Do not be afraid, for I know that you
are looking for Jesus, who was crucified. 6 He is not here; he has
risen, just as he said. Come and see the place where he lay. 7 Then
go quickly and tell his disciples: 'He has risen from the dead and is
going ahead of you into Galilee. There you will see him.' Now I have
told you."

8 So the women hurried away from the tomb, afraid yet filled with
joy, and ran to tell his disciples. 9 Suddenly Jesus met
them. "Greetings," he said. They came to him, clasped his feet and
worshiped him. 10 Then Jesus said to them, "Do not be afraid. Go
and tell my brothers to go to Galilee; there they will see me."

11 While the women were on their way, some of the guards went
into the city and reported to the chief priests everything that had
happened. 12 When the chief priests had met with the elders and
devised a plan, they gave the soldiers a large sum of
money, 13 telling them, "You are to say, 'His disciples came during
the night and stole him away while we were asleep.' 14 If this report
gets to the governor, we will satisfy him and keep you out of
trouble." 15 So the soldiers took the money and did as they were
instructed. And this story has been widely circulated among the Jews
to this very day. 16 Then the eleven disciples went to Galilee, to the
mountain where Jesus had told them to go. 17 When they saw him,
they worshiped him; but some doubted.18 Then Jesus came to them
and said, "All authority in heaven and on earth has been given to
me. 19 Therefore go and make disciples of all nations, baptizing
them in the name of the Father and of the Son and of the Holy
Spirit, 20 and teaching them to obey everything I have commanded
you. And surely, I am with you always, to the very end of the age."

The Trial of Jesus of Nazareth

Mark 15:1-15

Very early in the morning, the chief priests, with
the elders, the teachers of the law and the
whole Sanhedrin, made their plans.
So, they bound Jesus, led him away and
handed him over to Pilate.
2 "Are you the king of the Jews?" asked Pilate.
"You have said so," Jesus replied.
3 The chief priests accused him of many
things. 4 So again Pilate asked him, "Aren't you
going to answer? See how many things they
are accusing you of."
5 But Jesus still made no reply, and Pilate was
amazed.

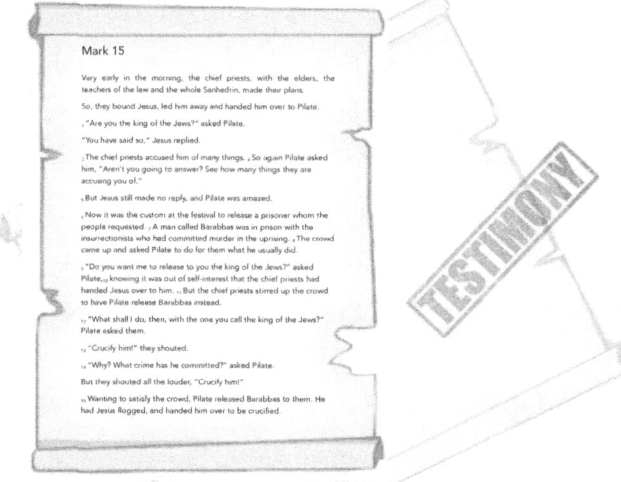
Mark 15

Very early in the morning, the chief priests, with the elders, the teachers of the law and the whole Sanhedrin, made their plans.

So, they bound Jesus, led him away and handed him over to Pilate.

2 "Are you the king of the Jews?" asked Pilate.

"You have said so," Jesus replied.

3 The chief priests accused him of many things. 4 So again Pilate asked him, "Aren't you going to answer? See how many things they are accusing you of."

5 But Jesus still made no reply, and Pilate was amazed.

6 Now it was the custom at the festival to release a prisoner whom the people requested. 7 A man called Barabbas was in prison with the insurrectionists who had committed murder in the uprising. 8 The crowd came up and asked Pilate to do for them what he usually did.

9 "Do you want me to release to you the king of the Jews?" asked Pilate, 10 knowing it was out of self-interest that the chief priests had handed Jesus over to him. 11 But the chief priests stirred up the crowd to have Pilate release Barabbas instead.

12 "What shall I do, then, with the one you call the king of the Jews?" Pilate asked them.

13 "Crucify him!" they shouted.

14 "Why? What crime has he committed?" asked Pilate.

But they shouted all the louder, "Crucify him!"

15 Wanting to satisfy the crowd, Pilate released Barabbas to them. He had Jesus flogged, and handed him over to be crucified.

6 Now it was the custom at the festival to
release a prisoner whom the people
requested. 7 A man called Barabbas was in
prison with the insurrectionists who had
committed murder in the uprising. 8 The crowd
came up and asked Pilate to do for them what
he usually did.
9 "Do you want me to release to you the king
of the Jews?" asked Pilate,10 knowing it was
out of self-interest that the chief priests had
handed Jesus over to him. 11 But the chief
priests stirred up the crowd to have Pilate
release Barabbas instead.
12 "What shall I do, then, with the one you call
the king of the Jews?" Pilate asked them.
13 "Crucify him!" they shouted.
14 "Why? What crime has he committed?"
asked Pilate.
But they shouted all the louder, "Crucify him!"
15 Wanting to satisfy the crowd, Pilate released
Barabbas to them. He had Jesus flogged, and
handed him over to be crucified.

The Trial of Jesus of Nazareth

Matthew 15:16-35

16 The soldiers led Jesus away into the palace (that is, the Praetorium) and called together the whole company of soldiers. 17 They put a purple robe on him, then twisted together a crown of thorns and set it on him. 18 And they began to call out to him, "Hail, king of the Jews!" 19 Again and again they struck him on the head with a staff and spit on him. Falling on their knees, they paid homage to him.

20 And when they had mocked him, they took off the purple robe and put his own clothes on him. Then they led him out to crucify him. 21 A certain man from Cyrene, Simon, the father of Alexander and Rufus, was passing by on his way in from the country, and they forced him to carry the cross.

22 They brought Jesus to the place called Golgotha (which means "the place of the skull"). 23 Then they offered him wine mixed with myrrh, but he did not take it.

24 And they crucified him. Dividing up his clothes, they cast lots to see what each would get. 25 It was nine in the morning when they crucified him. 26 The written notice of the charge against him read: the King of the Jews.

27 They crucified two rebels with him, one on his right and one on his left. Those who passed by hurled insults at him, shaking their heads and saying, "So! You who are going to destroy the temple and build it in three days, 30 come down from the cross and save yourself!" 31 In the same way the chief priests and the teachers of the law mocked him among themselves. "He saved others," they said, "but he can't save himself!

32 Let this Messiah, this king of Israel, come down now from the cross, that we may see and believe." Those crucified with him also heaped insults on him.

33 At noon, darkness came over the whole land until three in the afternoon. 34 And at three in the afternoon Jesus cried out in a loud voice, "Eloi, Eloi, lema sabachthani?" (which means "My God, my God, why have you forsaken me?").
35 When some of those standing near heard this, they said, "Listen, he's calling Elijah."

The Trial of Jesus of Nazareth

Matthew 15:36-47

Someone ran, filled a sponge with wine
vinegar, put it on a staff, and offered it to Jesus
to drink. "Now leave him alone. Let's see if
Elijah comes to take him down," he said.

37 With a loud cry, Jesus breathed his last.

38 The curtain of the temple was torn in two
from top to bottom. 39 And when the
centurion, who stood there in front of Jesus,
saw how he died, he said, "Surely this man was
the Son of God!"

40 Some women were watching from a
distance. Among them were Mary Magdalene,
Mary the mother of James the younger and of
Joseph, and Salome. 41 In Galilee these
women had followed him and cared for his
needs. Many other women who had come up
with him to Jerusalem were also there.

42 It was Preparation Day (that is, the day
before the Sabbath). So, as evening
approached, 43 Joseph of Arimathea, a
prominent member of the Council, who was
himself waiting for the kingdom of God, went
boldly to Pilate and asked for Jesus' body.

44 Pilate was surprised to hear that he was
already dead. Summoning the centurion, he
asked him if Jesus had already died. 45 When
he learned from the centurion that it was so, he
gave the body to Joseph.

46 So Joseph bought some linen cloth, took
down the body, wrapped it in the linen, and
placed it in a tomb cut out of rock. Then he
rolled a stone against the entrance of the
tomb. 47 Mary Magdalene and Mary the
mother of Joseph saw where he was laid.

Mark 16:1-8

When the Sabbath was over, Mary Magdalene,
Mary the mother of James, and Salome bought
spices so that they might go to anoint Jesus'
body. 2 Very early on the first day of the week,
just after sunrise, they were on their way to the
tomb 3 and they asked each other, "Who will
roll the stone away from the entrance of the
tomb?"

4 But when they looked up, they saw that the
stone, which was very large, had been rolled
away. 5 As they entered the tomb, they saw a
young man dressed in a white robe sitting on
the right side, and they were alarmed.

6 "Don't be alarmed," he said. "You are
looking for Jesus the Nazarene, who was
crucified. He has risen! He is not here. See the
place where they laid him. 7 But go, tell his
disciples and Peter, 'He is going ahead of you
into Galilee. There you will see him, just as he
told you.'"

8 Trembling and bewildered, the women went
out and fled from the tomb. They said nothing
to anyone, because they were afraid.

Textual Evidence (What is the reference)	Evidence Quote (Key Words)	Evidence in my own words (Summary)

The Trial of Jesus of Nazareth

Luke 23:1-16

Then the whole assembly rose and led him off
to Pilate. 2 And they began to accuse him,
saying, "We have found this man subverting
our nation. He opposes payment of taxes to
Caesar and claims to be Messiah, a king."
3 So Pilate asked Jesus, "Are you the king of
the Jews?"
"You have said so," Jesus replied.
4 Then Pilate announced to the chief priests
and the crowd, "I find no basis for a charge
against this man."
5 But they insisted, "He stirs up the people all
over Judea by his teaching. He started in
Galilee and has come all the way here."

6 On hearing this, Pilate asked if the man was a
Galilean. 7 When he learned that Jesus was
under Herod's jurisdiction, he sent him to
Herod, who was also in Jerusalem at that time.
8 When Herod saw Jesus, he was greatly
pleased, because for a long time he had been
wanting to see him. From what he had heard
about him, he hoped to see him perform a sign
of some sort. 9 He plied him with many
questions, but Jesus gave him no answer.

10 The chief priests and the teachers of the law
were standing there, vehemently accusing
him. 11 Then Herod and his soldiers ridiculed
and mocked him. Dressing him in an elegant
robe, they sent him back to Pilate. 12 That day
Herod and Pilate became friends—before this
they had been enemies.

13 Pilate called together the chief priests, the
rulers and the people, 14 and said to them,
"You brought me this man as one who was
inciting the people to rebellion. I have
examined him in your presence and have found
no basis for your charges against
him. 15 Neither has Herod, for he sent him
back to us; as you can see, he has done nothing
to deserve death. 16 Therefore, I will punish
him and then release him."

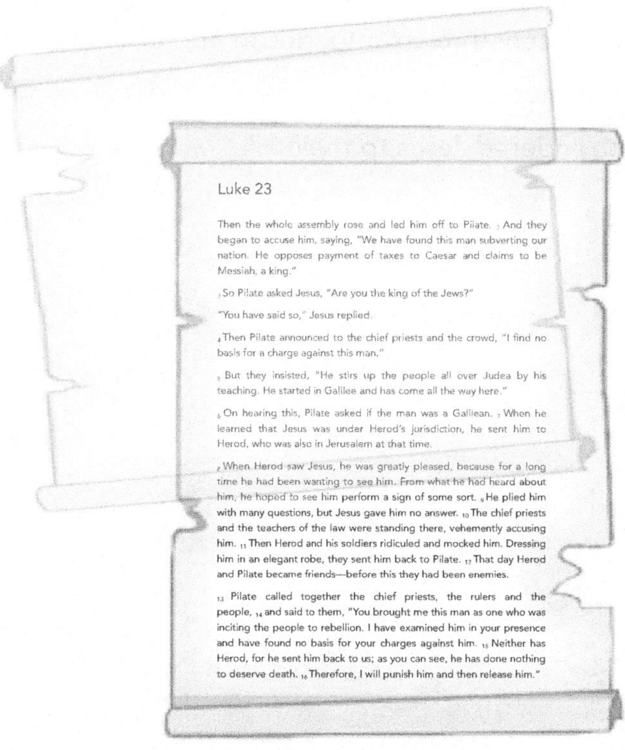

Luke 23

Then the whole assembly rose and led him off to Pilate. 2 And they began to accuse him, saying, "We have found this man subverting our nation. He opposes payment of taxes to Caesar and claims to be Messiah, a king."

3 So Pilate asked Jesus, "Are you the king of the Jews?"

"You have said so," Jesus replied.

4 Then Pilate announced to the chief priests and the crowd, "I find no basis for a charge against this man."

5 But they insisted, "He stirs up the people all over Judea by his teaching. He started in Galilee and has come all the way here."

6 On hearing this, Pilate asked if the man was a Galilean. 7 When he learned that Jesus was under Herod's jurisdiction, he sent him to Herod, who was also in Jerusalem at that time.

8 When Herod saw Jesus, he was greatly pleased, because for a long time he had been wanting to see him. From what he had heard about him, he hoped to see him perform a sign of some sort. 9 He plied him with many questions, but Jesus gave him no answer. 10 The chief priests and the teachers of the law were standing there, vehemently accusing him. 11 Then Herod and his soldiers ridiculed and mocked him. Dressing him in an elegant robe, they sent him back to Pilate. 12 That day Herod and Pilate became friends—before this they had been enemies.

13 Pilate called together the chief priests, the rulers and the people, 14 and said to them, "You brought me this man as one who was inciting the people to rebellion. I have examined him in your presence and have found no basis for your charges against him. 15 Neither has Herod, for he sent him back to us; as you can see, he has done nothing to deserve death. 16 Therefore, I will punish him and then release him."

The Trial of Jesus of Nazareth

Luke 23:18-33

18 But the whole crowd shouted, "Away with
this man! Release Barabbas to us!"19 (Barabbas
had been thrown into prison for an insurrection
in the city, and for murder.) 20 Wanting to
release Jesus, Pilate appealed to them
again. 21 But they kept shouting, "Crucify him!
Crucify him!"

22 For the third time he spoke to them: "Why?
What crime has this man committed? I have
found in him no grounds for the death penalty.
Therefore, I will have him punished and then
release him."

23 But with loud shouts they insistently
demanded that he be crucified, and their
shouts prevailed. 24 So Pilate decided to grant
their demand. 25 He released the man who
had been thrown into prison for insurrection
and murder, the one they asked for, and
surrendered Jesus to their will.

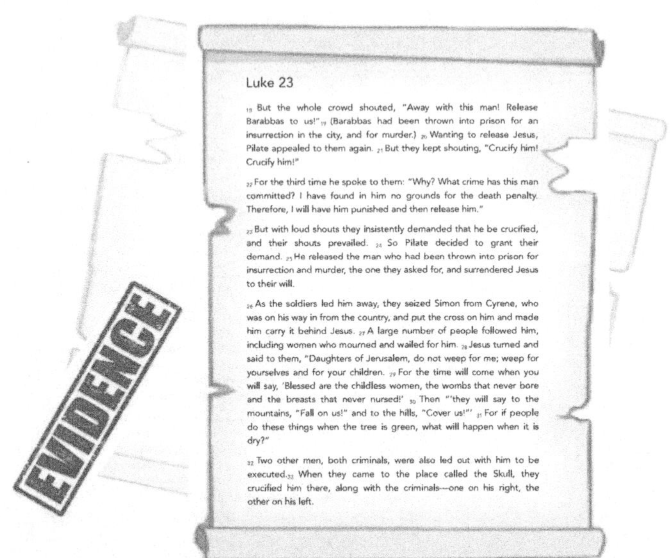

Luke 23

18 But the whole crowd shouted, "Away with this man! Release Barabbas to us!" 19 (Barabbas had been thrown into prison for an insurrection in the city, and for murder.) 20 Wanting to release Jesus, Pilate appealed to them again. 21 But they kept shouting, "Crucify him! Crucify him!"

22 For the third time he spoke to them: "Why? What crime has this man committed? I have found in him no grounds for the death penalty. Therefore, I will have him punished and then release him."

23 But with loud shouts they insistently demanded that he be crucified, and their shouts prevailed. 24 So Pilate decided to grant their demand. 25 He released the man who had been thrown into prison for insurrection and murder, the one they asked for, and surrendered Jesus to their will.

26 As the soldiers led him away, they seized Simon from Cyrene, who was on his way in from the country, and put the cross on him and made him carry it behind Jesus. 27 A large number of people followed him, including women who mourned and wailed for him. 28 Jesus turned and said to them, "Daughters of Jerusalem, do not weep for me; weep for yourselves and for your children. 29 For the time will come when you will say, 'Blessed are the childless women, the wombs that never bore and the breasts that never nursed!' 30 Then "'they will say to the mountains, "Fall on us!" and to the hills, "Cover us!"' 31 For if people do these things when the tree is green, what will happen when it is dry?"

32 Two other men, both criminals, were also led out with him to be executed. 33 When they came to the place called the Skull, they crucified him there, along with the criminals—one on his right, the other on his left.

26 As the soldiers led him away, they seized
Simon from Cyrene, who was on his way in
from the country, and put the cross on him and
made him carry it behind Jesus.

27 A large number of people followed him,
including women who mourned and wailed for
him. 28 Jesus turned and said to
them, "Daughters of Jerusalem, do not weep
for me; weep for yourselves and for your
children. 29 For the time will come when you
will say, 'Blessed are the childless women, the
wombs that never bore and the breasts that
never nursed!'

30 Then "'they will say to the mountains, "Fall
on us!" and to the hills, "Cover us!"' 31 For if
people do these things when the tree is green,
what will happen when it is dry?"

32 Two other men, both criminals, were also
led out with him to be executed. 33 When they
came to the place called the Skull, they
crucified him there, along with the criminals—
one on his right, the other on his left.

The Trial of Jesus of Nazareth

Luke 23:34-49

34 Jesus said, "Father, forgive them, for they
do not know what they are doing." And they
divided up his clothes by casting lots. 35 The
people stood watching, and the rulers even
sneered at him. They said, "He saved others;
let him save himself if he is God's Messiah, the
Chosen One."

36 The soldiers also came up and mocked
him. They offered him wine vinegar37 and said,
"If you are the king of the Jews, save yourself."

38 There was a written notice above him, which
read: this is the king of the Jews.

39 One of the criminals who hung there hurled
insults at him: "Aren't you the Messiah? Save
yourself and us!"

40 But the other criminal rebuked him. "Don't
you fear God," he said, "since you are under
the same sentence? 41 We are punished justly,
for we are getting what our deeds deserve. But
this man has done nothing wrong."

42 Then he said, "Jesus, remember me when
you come into your kingdom." 43 Jesus
answered him, "Truly I tell you, today you will
be with me in paradise." 44 It was now about
noon, and darkness came over the whole land
until three in the afternoon, 45 for the sun
stopped shining. And the curtain of the
temple was torn in two. 46 Jesus called out
with a loud voice, "Father, into your hands I
commit my spirit."[e] When he had said this, he
breathed his last. 47 The centurion, seeing
what had happened, praised God and said,
"Surely this was a righteous man." 48 When all
the people who had gathered to witness this
sight saw what took place, they beat their
breasts and went away. 49 But all those who
knew him, including the women who had
followed him from Galilee, stood at a
distance, watching these things.

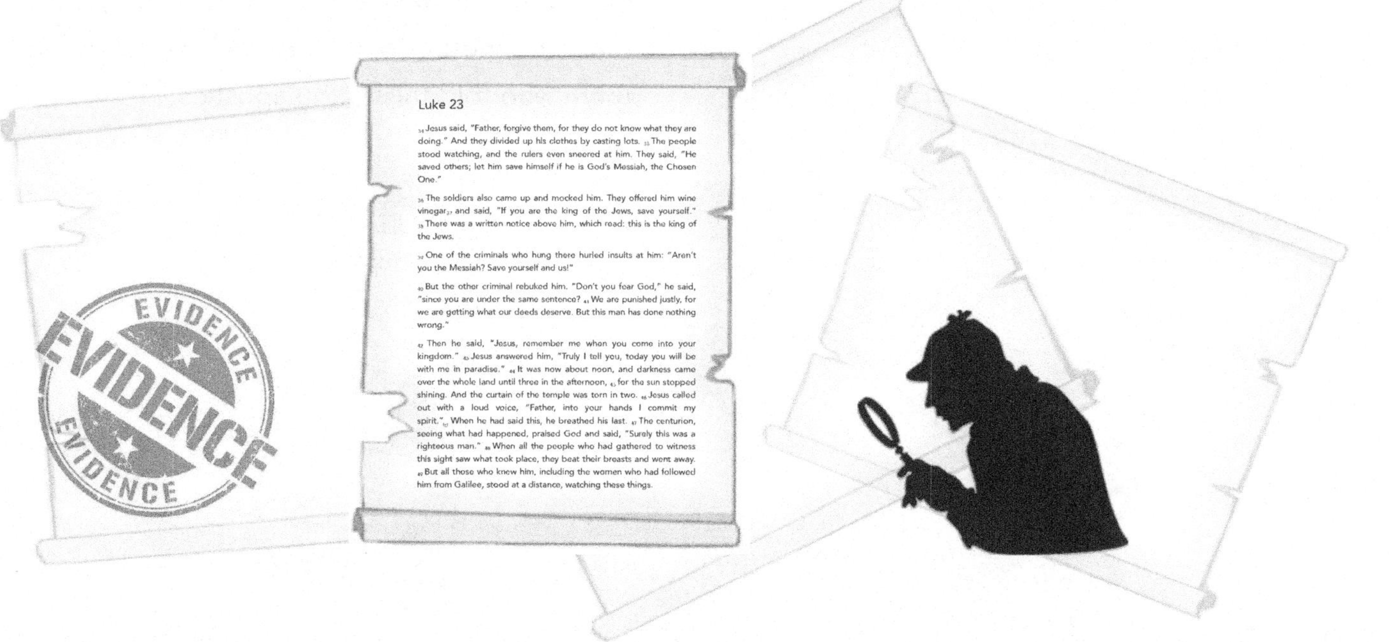

The Trial of Jesus of Nazareth

Luke 23:50-56

50 Now there was a man named Joseph, a member of the Council, a good and upright man, 51 who had not consented to their decision and action. He came from the Judean town of Arimathea, and he himself was waiting for the kingdom of God. 52 Going to Pilate, he asked for Jesus' body. 53 Then he took it down, wrapped it in linen cloth and placed it in a tomb cut in the rock, one in which no one had yet been laid. 54 It was Preparation Day, and the Sabbath was about to begin. 55 The women who had come with Jesus from Galilee followed Joseph and saw the tomb and how his body was laid in it. 56 Then they went home and prepared spices and perfumes. But they rested on the Sabbath in obedience to the commandment.

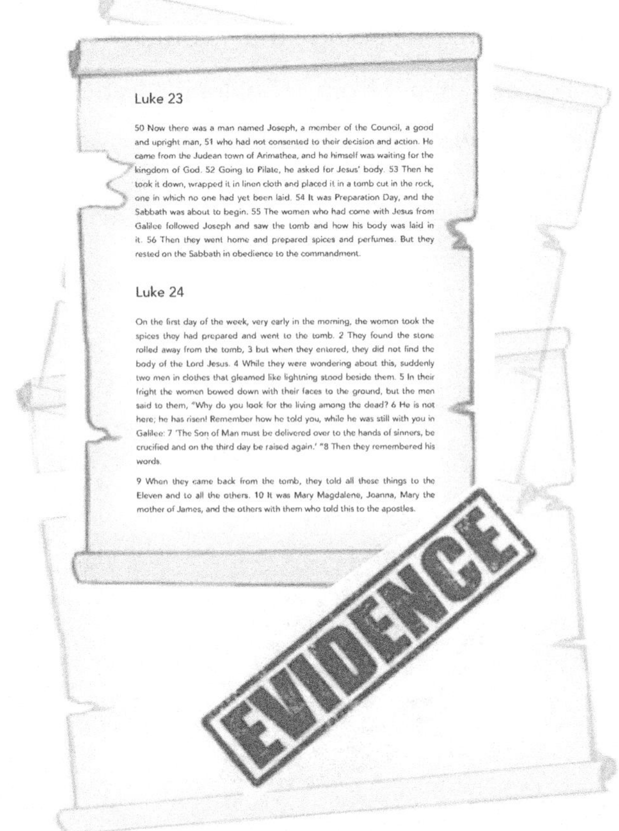
Luke 23

50 Now there was a man named Joseph, a member of the Council, a good and upright man, 51 who had not consented to their decision and action. He came from the Judean town of Arimathea, and he himself was waiting for the kingdom of God. 52 Going to Pilate, he asked for Jesus' body. 53 Then he took it down, wrapped it in linen cloth and placed it in a tomb cut in the rock, one in which no one had yet been laid. 54 It was Preparation Day, and the Sabbath was about to begin. 55 The women who had come with Jesus from Galilee followed Joseph and saw the tomb and how his body was laid in it. 56 Then they went home and prepared spices and perfumes. But they rested on the Sabbath in obedience to the commandment.

Luke 24

On the first day of the week, very early in the morning, the women took the spices they had prepared and went to the tomb. 2 They found the stone rolled away from the tomb, 3 but when they entered, they did not find the body of the Lord Jesus. 4 While they were wondering about this, suddenly two men in clothes that gleamed like lightning stood beside them. 5 In their fright the women bowed down with their faces to the ground, but the men said to them, "Why do you look for the living among the dead? 6 He is not here; he has risen! Remember how he told you, while he was still with you in Galilee: 7 'The Son of Man must be delivered over to the hands of sinners, be crucified and on the third day be raised again.' "8 Then they remembered his words.

9 When they came back from the tomb, they told all these things to the Eleven and to all the others. 10 It was Mary Magdalene, Joanna, Mary the mother of James, and the others with them who told this to the apostles.

Luke 24:1-10

On the first day of the week, very early in the morning, the women took the spices they had prepared and went to the tomb. 2 They found the stone rolled away from the tomb, 3 but when they entered, they did not find the body of the Lord Jesus. 4 While they were wondering about this, suddenly two men in clothes that gleamed like lightning stood beside them. 5 In their fright the women bowed down with their faces to the ground, but the men said to them, "Why do you look for the living among the dead? 6 He is not here; he has risen! Remember how he told you, while he was still with you in Galilee: 7 'The Son of Man must be delivered over to the hands of sinners, be crucified and on the third day be raised again.' "8 Then they remembered his words.

9 When they came back from the tomb, they told all these things to the Eleven and to all the others. 10 It was Mary Magdalene, Joanna, Mary the mother of James, and the others with them who told this to the apostles.

The Trial of Jesus of Nazareth

Luke 24:11-26

But they did not believe the women, because their words seemed to them like nonsense. 12 Peter, however, got up and ran to the tomb. Bending over, he saw the strips of linen lying by themselves, and he went away, wondering to himself what had happened.

13 Now that same day two of them were going to a village called Emmaus, about seven miles from Jerusalem. 14 They were talking with each other about everything that had happened. 15 As they talked and discussed these things with each other, Jesus himself came up and walked along with them; 16 but they were kept from recognizing him.

17 He asked them, "What are you discussing together as you walk along?"

They stood still, their faces downcast. 18 One of them, named Cleopas, asked him, "Are you the only one visiting Jerusalem who does not know the things that have happened there in these days?"

19 "What things?" he asked.

"About Jesus of Nazareth," they replied. "He was a prophet, powerful in word and deed before God and all the people. 20 The chief priests and our rulers handed him over to be sentenced to death, and they crucified him; 21 but we had hoped that he was the one who was going to redeem Israel. And what is more, it is the third day since all this took place. 22 In addition, some of our women amazed us. They went to the tomb early this morning 23 but didn't find his body. They came and told us that they had seen a vision of angels, who said he was alive. 24 Then some of our companions went to the tomb and found it just as the women had said, but they did not see Jesus."

25 He said to them, "How foolish you are, and how slow to believe all that the prophets have spoken! 26 Did not the Messiah have to suffer these things and then enter his glory?"

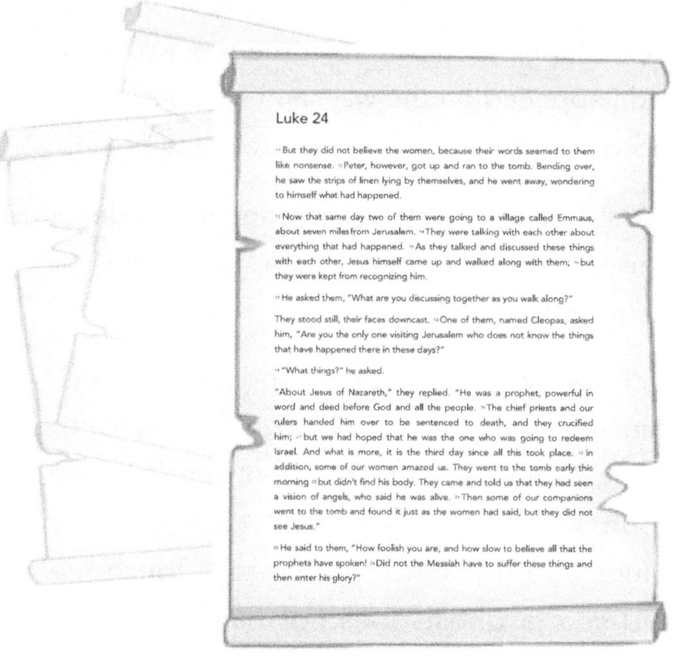
Luke 24

11 But they did not believe the women, because their words seemed to them like nonsense. 12 Peter, however, got up and ran to the tomb. Bending over, he saw the strips of linen lying by themselves, and he went away, wondering to himself what had happened.

13 Now that same day two of them were going to a village called Emmaus, about seven miles from Jerusalem. 14 They were talking with each other about everything that had happened. 15 As they talked and discussed these things with each other, Jesus himself came up and walked along with them; 16 but they were kept from recognizing him.

17 He asked them, "What are you discussing together as you walk along?"

They stood still, their faces downcast. 18 One of them, named Cleopas, asked him, "Are you the only one visiting Jerusalem who does not know the things that have happened there in these days?"

19 "What things?" he asked.

"About Jesus of Nazareth," they replied. "He was a prophet, powerful in word and deed before God and all the people. 20 The chief priests and our rulers handed him over to be sentenced to death, and they crucified him; 21 but we had hoped that he was the one who was going to redeem Israel. And what is more, it is the third day since all this took place. 22 In addition, some of our women amazed us. They went to the tomb early this morning 23 but didn't find his body. They came and told us that they had seen a vision of angels, who said he was alive. 24 Then some of our companions went to the tomb and found it just as the women had said, but they did not see Jesus."

25 He said to them, "How foolish you are, and how slow to believe all that the prophets have spoken! 26 Did not the Messiah have to suffer these things and then enter his glory?"

The Trial of Jesus of Nazareth

Luke 23:27-53

27 And beginning with Moses and all the
Prophets, he explained to them what was said
in all the Scriptures concerning himself.

28 As they approached the village to which they
were going, Jesus continued on as if he were
going farther. 29 But they urged him strongly,
"Stay with us, for it is nearly evening; the day is
almost over." So he went in to stay with them.

30 When he was at the table with them, he took
bread, gave thanks, broke it and began to give
it to them. 31 Then their eyes were opened and
they recognized him, and he disappeared from
their sight. 32 They asked each other, "Were not
our hearts burning within us while he talked
with us on the road and opened the
Scriptures to us?"

33 They got up and returned at once to
Jerusalem. There they found the Eleven and
those with them, assembled together 34 and
saying, "It is true! The Lord has risen and has
appeared to Simon." 35 Then the two told what
had happened on the way, and how Jesus was
recognized by them when he broke the bread.

36 While they were still talking about this, Jesus
himself stood among them and said to
them, "Peace be with you."

37 They were startled and frightened,
thinking they saw a ghost. 38 He said to
them, "Why are you troubled, and why do
doubts rise in your minds? 39 Look at my
hands and my feet. It is I myself! Touch me
and see; a ghost does not have flesh and
bones, as you see I have."

40 When he had said this, he showed them his
hands and feet. 41 And while they still did not
believe it because of joy and amazement, he
asked them, "Do you have anything here to
eat?" 42 They gave him a piece of broiled
fish, 43 and he took it and ate it in their
presence.

44 He said to them, "This is what I told you while
I was still with you: Everything must be
fulfilled that is written about me in the Law of
Moses, the Prophets and the Psalms."

45 Then he opened their minds so they could
understand the Scriptures. 46 He told
them, "This is what is written: The Messiah will
suffer and rise from the dead on the third
day, 47 and repentance for the forgiveness of
sins will be preached in his name to all
nations, beginning at Jerusalem. 48 You are
witnesses of these things. 49 I am going to send
you what my Father has promised; but stay in
the city until you have been clothed with power
from on high."

50 When he had led them out to the vicinity of
Bethany, he lifted up his hands and blessed
them. 51 While he was blessing them, he left
them and was taken up into heaven. 52 Then
they worshiped him and returned to Jerusalem
with great joy. 53 And they stayed continually at
the temple, praising God.

Textual Evidence (What is the reference)	Evidence Quote (Key Words)	Evidence in my own words (Summary)

Notes:

The Trial of Jesus of Nazareth

John 19:1-14

Then Pilate took Jesus and had him flogged. 2 The soldiers twisted together a crown of thorns and put it on his head. They clothed him in a purple robe 3 and went up to him again and again, saying, "Hail, king of the Jews!" And they slapped him in the face.

4 Once more Pilate came out and said to the Jews gathered there, "Look, I am bringing him out to you to let you know that I find no basis for a charge against him." 5 When Jesus came out wearing the crown of thorns and the purple robe, Pilate said to them, "Here is the man!"

6 As soon as the chief priests and their officials saw him, they shouted, "Crucify! Crucify!"

But Pilate answered, "You take him and crucify him. As for me, I find no basis for a charge against him."

7 The Jewish leaders insisted, "We have a law, and according to that law he must die, because he claimed to be the Son of God."

8 When Pilate heard this, he was even more afraid, 9 and he went back inside the palace. "Where do you come from?" he asked Jesus, but Jesus gave him no answer. 10 "Do you refuse to speak to me?" Pilate said. "Don't you realize I have power either to free you or to crucify you?"

11 Jesus answered, "You would have no power over me if it were not given to you from above. Therefore, the one who handed me over to you is guilty of a greater sin."

12 From then on, Pilate tried to set Jesus free, but the Jewish leaders kept shouting, "If you let this man go, you are no friend of Caesar. Anyone who claims to be a king opposes Caesar."

13 When Pilate heard this, he brought Jesus out and sat down on the judge's seat at a place known as the Stone Pavement (which in Aramaic is Gabbatha). 14 It was the day of Preparation of the Passover; it was about noon.

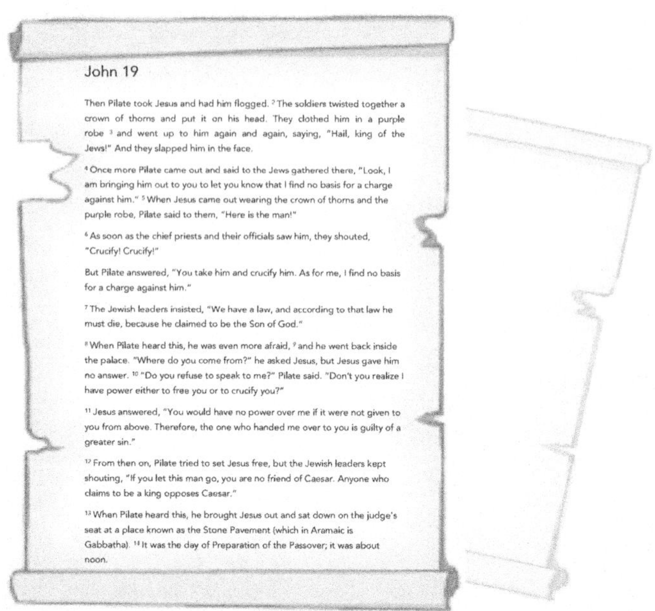

John 19

Then Pilate took Jesus and had him flogged. 2 The soldiers twisted together a crown of thorns and put it on his head. They clothed him in a purple robe 3 and went up to him again and again, saying, "Hail, king of the Jews!" And they slapped him in the face.

4 Once more Pilate came out and said to the Jews gathered there, "Look, I am bringing him out to you to let you know that I find no basis for a charge against him." 5 When Jesus came out wearing the crown of thorns and the purple robe, Pilate said to them, "Here is the man!"

6 As soon as the chief priests and their officials saw him, they shouted, "Crucify! Crucify!"

But Pilate answered, "You take him and crucify him. As for me, I find no basis for a charge against him."

7 The Jewish leaders insisted, "We have a law, and according to that law he must die, because he claimed to be the Son of God."

8 When Pilate heard this, he was even more afraid, 9 and he went back inside the palace. "Where do you come from?" he asked Jesus, but Jesus gave him no answer. 10 "Do you refuse to speak to me?" Pilate said. "Don't you realize I have power either to free you or to crucify you?"

11 Jesus answered, "You would have no power over me if it were not given to you from above. Therefore, the one who handed me over to you is guilty of a greater sin."

12 From then on, Pilate tried to set Jesus free, but the Jewish leaders kept shouting, "If you let this man go, you are no friend of Caesar. Anyone who claims to be a king opposes Caesar."

13 When Pilate heard this, he brought Jesus out and sat down on the judge's seat at a place known as the Stone Pavement (which in Aramaic is Gabbatha). 14 It was the day of Preparation of the Passover; it was about noon.

The Trial of Jesus of Nazareth

John 20:1-15

Early on the first day of the week, while it was still dark, Mary Magdalene went to the tomb and saw that the stone had been removed from the entrance.2 So she came running to Simon Peter and the other disciple, the one Jesus loved, and said, "They have taken the Lord out of the tomb, and we don't know where they have put him!"

3 So Peter and the other disciple started for the tomb. 4 Both were running, but the other disciple outran Peter and reached the tomb first. 5 He bent over and looked in at the strips of linen lying there but did not go in. 6 Then Simon Peter came along behind him and went straight into the tomb. He saw the strips of linen lying there, 7 as well as the cloth that had been wrapped around Jesus' head. The cloth was still lying in its place, separate from the linen.

8 Finally the other disciple, who had reached the tomb first, also went inside. He saw and believed. 9 (They still did not understand from Scripture that Jesus had to rise from the dead.) 10 Then the disciples went back to where they were staying.

11 Now Mary stood outside the tomb crying. As she wept, she bent over to look into the tomb 12 and saw two angels in white, seated where Jesus' body had been, one at the head and the other at the foot. 13 They asked her, "Woman, why are you crying?"

"They have taken my Lord away," she said, "and I don't know where they have put him." 14 At this, she turned around and saw Jesus standing there, but she did not realize that it was Jesus.

15 He asked her, "Woman, why are you crying? Who is it you are looking for?"

Thinking he was the gardener, she said, "Sir, if you have carried him away, tell me where you have put him, and I will get him."

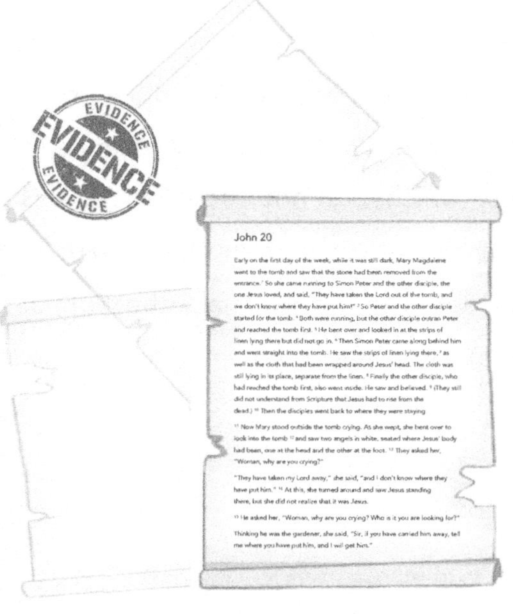

John 20

Early on the first day of the week, while it was still dark, Mary Magdalene went to the tomb and saw that the stone had been removed from the entrance.2 So she came running to Simon Peter and the other disciple, the one Jesus loved, and said, "They have taken the Lord out of the tomb, and we don't know where they have put him!" 3 So Peter and the other disciple started for the tomb. 4 Both were running, but the other disciple outran Peter and reached the tomb first. 5 He bent over and looked in at the strips of linen lying there but did not go in. 6 Then Simon Peter came along behind him and went straight into the tomb. He saw the strips of linen lying there, 7 as well as the cloth that had been wrapped around Jesus' head. The cloth was still lying in its place, separate from the linen. 8 Finally the other disciple, who had reached the tomb first, also went inside. He saw and believed. 9 (They still did not understand from Scripture that Jesus had to rise from the dead.) 10 Then the disciples went back to where they were staying

11 Now Mary stood outside the tomb crying. As she wept, she bent over to look into the tomb 12 and saw two angels in white, seated where Jesus' body had been, one at the head and the other at the foot. 13 They asked her, "Woman, why are you crying?"

"They have taken my Lord away," she said, "and I don't know where they have put him." 14 At this, she turned around and saw Jesus standing there, but she did not realize that it was Jesus.

15 He asked her, "Woman, why are you crying? Who is it you are looking for?"

Thinking he was the gardener, she said, "Sir, if you have carried him away, tell me where you have put him, and I will get him."

The Trial of Jesus of Nazareth

John 20:16-31

16 Jesus said to her, "Mary."

She turned toward him and cried out in Aramaic, "Rabboni!" (which means "Teacher").

17 Jesus said, "Do not hold on to me, for I have not yet ascended to the Father. Go instead to my brothers and tell them, 'I am ascending to my Father and your Father, to my God and your God.'"

18 Mary Magdalene went to the disciples with the news: "I have seen the Lord!" And she told them that he had said these things to her.

19 On the evening of that first day of the week, when the disciples were together, with the doors locked for fear of the Jewish leaders, Jesus came and stood among them and said, "Peace be with you!" 20 After he said this, he showed them his hands and side. The disciples were overjoyed when they saw the Lord. 21 Again Jesus said, "Peace be with you! As the Father has sent me, I am sending you." 22 And with that he breathed on them and said, "Receive the Holy Spirit.

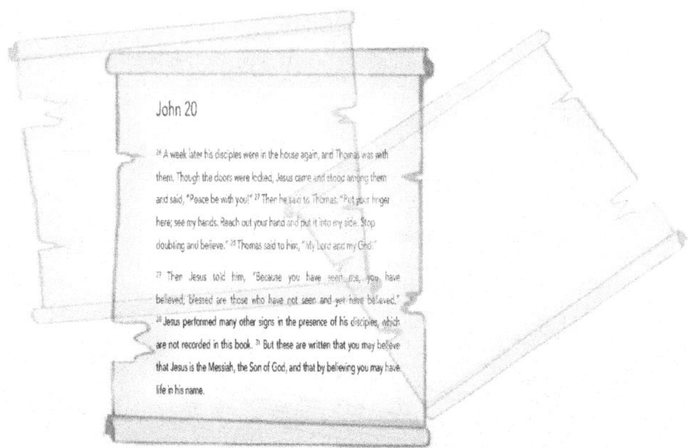

John 20

26 A week later his disciples were in the house again, and Thomas was with them. Though the doors were locked, Jesus came and stood among them and said, "Peace be with you!" 27 Then he said to Thomas, "Put your finger here; see my hands. Reach out your hand and put it into my side. Stop doubting and believe." 28 Thomas said to him, "My Lord and my God!"

29 Then Jesus told him, "Because you have seen me, you have believed; blessed are those who have not seen and yet have believed." 30 Jesus performed many other signs in the presence of his disciples, which are not recorded in this book. 31 But these are written that you may believe that Jesus is the Messiah, the Son of God, and that by believing you may have life in his name.

23 If you forgive anyone's sins, their sins are forgiven; if you do not forgive them, they are not forgiven." 24 Now Thomas (also known as Didymus), one of the Twelve, was not with the disciples when Jesus came. 25 So the other disciples told him, "We have seen the Lord!" But he said to them, "Unless I see the nail marks in his hands and put my finger where the nails were, and put my hand into his side, I will not believe."

26 A week later his disciples were in the house again, and Thomas was with them. Though the doors were locked, Jesus came and stood among them and said, "Peace be with you!" 27 Then he said to Thomas, "Put your finger here; see my hands. Reach out your hand and put it into my side. Stop doubting and believe." 28 Thomas said to him, "My Lord and my God!"

29 Then Jesus told him, "Because you have seen me, you have believed; blessed are those who have not seen and yet have believed." 30 Jesus performed many other signs in the presence of his disciples, which are not recorded in this book. 31 But these are written that you may believe that Jesus is the Messiah, the Son of God, and that by believing you may have life in his name.

Read like a Detective

Acts

God has raised this Jesus to life, and we are all witnesses of it.

Acts 2:32

You killed the author of life, but God raised him from the dead. We are witnesses of this.

Acts 3:15

"We are witnesses of everything he did in the country of the Jews and in Jerusalem. They killed him by hanging him on a cross,

Acts 10:39

He was not seen by all the people, but by witnesses whom God had already chosen—by us who ate and drank with him after he rose from the dead.

Acts 10:41

- Who said it?
- Where was it said?
- Who heard it?
- Why does it matter?

Did Jesus really rise from the dead?

Can I trust the resurrection story?

Textual Evidence *(What is the reference)*	***Evidence Quote*** *(Key Words)*	***Evidence in my own words*** *(Summary)*

Investigation Summary

To be Submitted by Authorized Agents Only
Do not submit this document if it is wet or damp.

EVIDENCE
EVIDENCE
EVIDENCE

Source of Evidence: ______________________________

Summary Description of Evidence:

Detective Evaluation

COLLABORATION RUBRIC

Notes and Plans:

	Below Standard	Approaching Standard	At Standard	Above Standard
Takes Personal Responsibility for Learning and Contributing to the Learning Process	• Is not prepared, informed or ready to contribute to the team • Does not utilize technology as agreed upon • Does not participate in project tasks • Does not listen to or use feedback to improve work	• Usually prepared, informed and ready to work with team • Does not utilize technology according to agreed upon standards with consistency • Needs reminding or prompting to complete tasks • Uses some feedback and complete most tasks	• Prepared and ready to work • Well informed and cites evidence that encourages learning among other team members • Consistently uses technology as agree upon • Self motivated and does not need to be reminded to complete tasks • Completes tasks on time • Evaluates and uses feedback to improve work	
Contribution to the Team	• Does not help the team to solve problems; may be the source of problems for the team • Does not ask probing questions, express ideas, or elaborate in response to questions or discussions • Do not offer help • Does not provide useful feedback	• Cooperates but does not actively participate in problem solving • Occasionally asks probing questions, expresses ideas, or elaborates in responses or discussions • Sometimes offers help • Sometimes provides feedback but it may not always be helpful	• Helps the team to solve problems and manage conflict • Clearly expresses ideas, asks probing questions, listens to others and solicits feedback from quiet team members to ensure that all perspectives are shared and heard • Provides useful feedback • Identifies opportunities to help others where appropriate	
Relationships and Respect	• Impolite or unkind to team members (may interrupt, ignore, talk over or use hurtful words or body language) • Does not listen or respect other perspectives	• Usually polite and kind to team members • Usually listens and respects team members • Disagrees with content, perspectives and opinions without attacking the person	• Polite and kind to team members • Listens to, acknowledges and respects other team members • Disagrees with content and builds community by affirming the person	

TRUE HERO

"The true story of the extraordinary mission of God"

pillar

Learning to love God's Word

Acts 2: 1–13, NASB

Pentecost

1 When the day of Pentecost had come, they were all together in one place. 2 And suddenly there came from heaven a noise like a violent rushing wind, and it filled the whole house where they were sitting. **3 And there appeared to them tongues as of fire distributing themselves, and they rested on each one of them. 4 And they were all filled with the Holy Spirit and began to speak with other tongues, as the Spirit was giving them utterance.**

5 Now there were Jews living in Jerusalem, devout men from every nation under heaven. 6 And when this sound occurred, the crowd came together, and were bewildered because each one of them was hearing them speak in his own language.

7 They were amazed and astonished, saying, "Why, are not all these who are speaking Galileans?

8 And how is it that we each hear them in our own language to which we were born? 9 Parthians and Medes and Elamites, and residents of Mesopotamia, Judea and Cappadocia, Pontus and Asia, 10 Phrygia and Pamphylia, Egypt and the districts of Libya around Cyrene, and visitors from Rome, both Jews and proselytes,

11 Cretans and Arabs—we hear them in our own tongues speaking of the mighty deeds of God." 12 And they all continued in amazement and great perplexity, saying to one another, "What does this mean?"

13 But others were mocking and saying, "They are full of sweet wine."

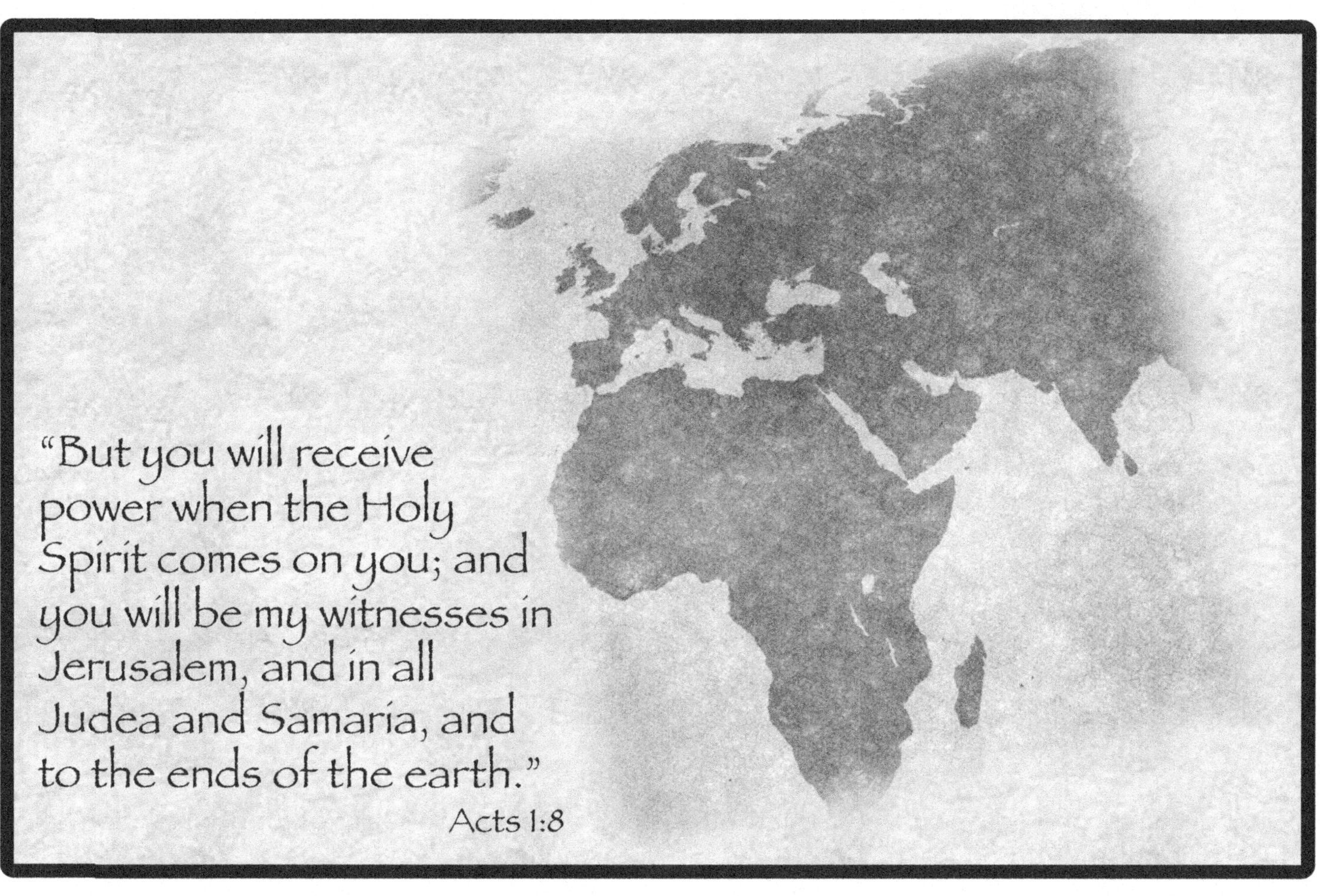

What happened at Pentecost?

How do a handful of disciples who just fifty days earlier abandoned the man that they claimed to be their Messiah during his moment of need become the ones who start a global movement in his name?

During Act I of the plot of Scripture, God gives His mission to Adam when he tells him to be fruitful, multiply and fill the earth with the reflection of the glory of God.

That same mission is repeated to Noah, Abraham, Isaac, Jacob, Moses, David, and Solomon.

Then after His resurrection from the dead, Jesus the Nazarene renews the mission of God to His disciples in a manner similar to how it is renewed again and again throughout the Hebrew Scriptures.

It was at Mount Sinai, during the feast of Pentecost (50 days after God delivered His people from their bondage in Egypt) that God wrote His law on tablets of stone.

Now, exactly 50 days after the deliverance of people from their bondage to sin, God pours out His Spirit and writes His commands on the hearts of His people.

At Sinai, 3,000 lose their lives. In Jerusalem, 3,000 are presented with the gift of eternal life.

PILLAR

How do I understand the role of Acts in the plot of Scripture?

What is the connection between Acts 2 and the Old Testament Threads?

PROLOGUE PATRIARCH PASSOVER PILLAR PROMISE PROXIMITY SHALOM

Each of the sermons in the book of Acts, whether they be from Peter, Stephen, or Paul, recognize the singular plot of Scripture. The Bible one story told in two Acts with seven scenes in each Act.

During the first scene of Act, I called the Prologue, where God introduces us to the mission of man to fill the earth with the reflection of God's glory. It is in the initial chapters that we learn of the rebellion of men and women against God, His glory, and His mission. Again and again, God demonstrates His grace and time, and again, we rebel in ever-increasing measures.

During the second scene of Act I, titled after the Patriarchs, we learn of God's intention to fulfill His mission through Abraham and his descendants. God makes an unconditional covenant and begins the process of fulfilling His promises.

During the third scene, the people of God are enslaved in Egypt, and God raises a deliverer who mediates between God, His people, and the Pharaoh who enslaves them. God demonstrates His power and authority over the false Egyptian gods and displays His glory to the nations through the events of the Passover.

Fifty days after their deliverance from bondage, God meets with His people at Mount Sinai, and His presence is manifest among them. In symbolism designed to invite His people to place Him in the center of their lives and visualize the Garden of Eden, the presence of God manifests itself in a Pillar. And throughout the fourth scene, we see God demonstrate His grace again and again to a people who are intent on rebelling against Him.

In scene 5, the see the faithfulness of God, and they enter the land that He had promised. But the integrity of their relationship does not last, and with each passing generation, the people pull further and further away from God and His purpose to reflect His glory to the nations of the world through His special relationship with them.

Near the end of scene 5, the people dedicate themselves to God in the presence of His temple. The temple was the place where all of the threads of Scripture converged, and we witnessed the place of God 's presence on earth, the place where people could be reconciled to Him and where all nations could see His glory. However, in scene 6, the people forget their covenant promise, and they rebel. Ultimately, God keeps His promise, and the people experience His discipline during their 70 years of exile.

Near the end of scene 5, the people dedicate themselves to God in the presence of His temple. The temple was the place where all of the threads of Scripture converged, and we witnessed the place of God 's presence on earth, the place where people could be reconciled to Him and where all nations could see His glory. However, in scene 6, the people forget their covenant promise, and they rebel. Ultimately, God keeps His promise, and the people experience His discipline during the 70 years of exile.

Act I ends with silence. For 400 years, His prophets do not speak the words, "this is the word of the Lord." It is not that God is not at work, but He is quiet. It is during this time that nations rise and fall. The Greeks pave the way for a common language among the nations. The Romans build a system of roads that safely connect the trade routes. And the people of God wait for the one He has promised will deliver them.

Then in the first scene of Act 2, God speaks and announces a new beginning. Messengers from God bring the good news and announce that the threads from Act I connect in the person of Jesus Christ.

Purple:

"they will call him Immanuel"(which means "God with us")."

Matthew 1:22

Gold:

"Glory to God in the Highest and on earth, peace good will to men."

Luke 2:14

Scarlet:

"you are to give him the name Jesus [Yeshua, which means God is salvation], because he will save his people from their sins."

Matthew 1:21

Connections between Act I and Act 2 become more obvious in the second scene as Jesus the Nazarene fulfills the promises of God through the prophets, reflects the glory of God and declares the Kingdom of God here on earth. Reminding us of Eden when Adam and Eve are filled with shame and hide from God, Jesus declares that He has come to seek and save those who are lost.

In the third scene, Christ completes the connection between the self-centered actions of Adam in the Garden of Eden (who words to God were not your will, but mine be done), and his own words in the Garden of Gethsemane when He stated, "not my will but yours be done." His unselfish act of obedience leads to His death on a cross followed by a demonstration of the power of God through His resurrection from the dead and the fulfillment of the scarlet thread.

But the story is not over. The story of the scarlet thread that began with the first pair of clothes in the Garden of Eden may have been fulfilled in the perfect act of substitution by Jesus Christ, but God's story is not complete. The Golden Thread has not been fulfilled, and with the return of Christ to heaven, the integrated connection between heaven and earth no longer exists.

How do I understand the role of Acts in the plot of Scripture?

God's story does not end with the Gospels. The story is not complete. The scarlet thread was fulfilled by the life, death, and resurrection of Christ, but the mission of God and the Golden Thread are not yet complete. The earth is not yet filled with the reflection of God's glory, and with the return of Christ to heaven, the integrated connection between heaven and earth no longer exists.

That is why the last words of Christ on earth are so crucial to understanding the plot.

In Matthew 28, Jesus tells those who are gathered to, "Go!" It is not an accident that Matthew would make one last Old Testament connection by beginning the instructions of Christ with the same word used to commission Abraham in Genesis 12. Then in a direct connection to God's words to Adam, Noah, Abraham, and those who followed, Jesus invites His followers to "go into all the world" and "make disciples."

But in the book of Acts, Luke writes the instructions of Christ as if they are a thesis or an outline to the history of the Church. In Acts 1:8, the words of Christ provide us and outline to the book of Acts.

> *"You will be my witnesses in Jerusalem, Judea, Samaria and the ends of the earth."*
>
> Jesus

Jerusalem (Acts 1-7)	Judea & Samaria (Acts 8-12)	**The ends of the earth** (Acts 13-28)
• The birth of the church among the Jews • Primary Witness: Peter and the 12	• The expansion of the church to the Gentiles • Primary Witness: Peter	• Jews and Gentiles work to reflect Christ to the nations • Primary Witness: Paul and his team

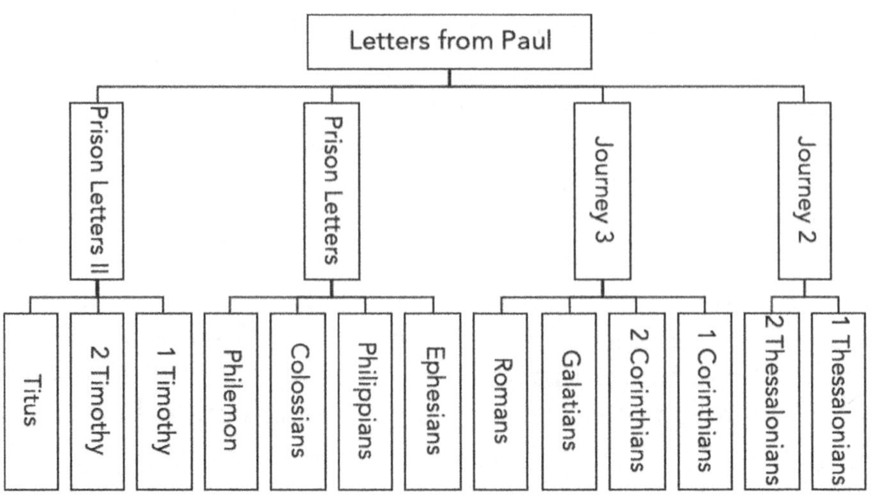

Near the end of scene 5 the people dedicate themselves to God in the presence of His temple.

Just the Facts

Book Name: Acts of the Apostles

Author: Dr. Luke (Personal Physician of Paul the Apostle)

Noteworthy: Acts is the second part of a two-part letter for Theophilus. In part I, the Gospel of Luke focuses on the life of Christ. In part 2, Acts focuses on life after Christ returns to heaven.

Acts is a historical book. Much like how the Gospels present the history of the life of Christ, Acts provides the history of the early church.

Notes:

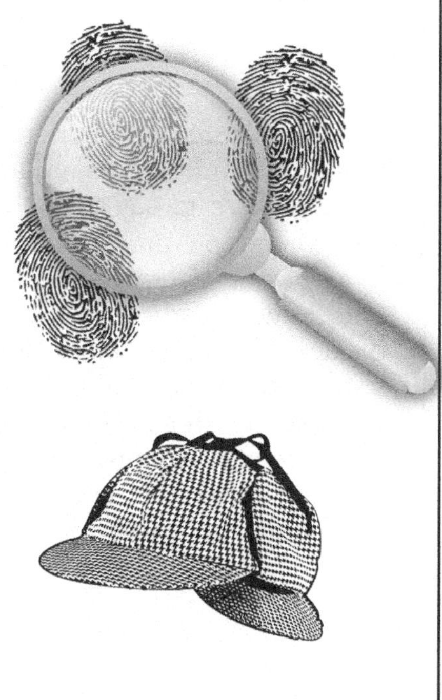

What happened at Pentecost?

What is the connection between Acts 2 and the Old Testament Threads?

34 Then the cloud covered the tent of
meeting, and the glory of the Lord filled
the tabernacle. 35 Moses could not enter
the tent of meeting because the cloud had
settled on it, and the glory of
the Lord filled the tabernacle.

36 In all the travels of the Israelites,
whenever the cloud lifted from above the
tabernacle, they would set out; 37 but if the
cloud did not lift, they did not set out—
until the day it lifted.

38 So the cloud of the Lord was over the
tabernacle by day, and fire was in the
cloud by night, in the sight of all the
Israelites during all their travels.

Exodus 40:34-38

When the day of Pentecost came, they were all
together in one place.2 Suddenly a sound like
the blowing of a violent wind came from heaven
and filled the whole house where they were
sitting. 3 They saw what seemed to be tongues
of fire that separated and came to rest on each
of them. 4 All of them were filled with the Holy
Spirit and began to speak in other tongues as
the Spirit enabled them.
5 Now there were staying in Jerusalem God-
fearing Jews from every nation under
heaven. 6 When they heard this sound, a crowd
came together in bewilderment, because each
one heard their own language being
spoken. 7 Utterly amazed, they asked: "Aren't all
these who are speaking Galileans? 8 Then how is
it that each of us hears them in our native
language? 9 Parthians, Medes and Elamites;
residents of Mesopotamia, Judea and
Cappadocia, Pontus and Asia,10 Phrygia and
Pamphylia, Egypt and the parts of Libya near
Cyrene; visitors from Rome 11 (both Jews and
converts to Judaism); Cretans and Arabs—we
hear them declaring the wonders of God in our
own tongues!" 12 Amazed and perplexed, they
asked one another, "What does this mean?"

Acts 2:1-12

3 Then Moses went up to God, and the LORD
called to him from the mountain and said, "This is
what you are to say to the descendants of Jacob
and what you are to tell the people of Israel:
4 'You yourselves have seen what I did to Egypt,
and how I carried you on eagles' wings and
brought you to myself. 5 Now if you obey me fully
and keep my covenant, then out of all nations you
will be my treasured possession. Although the
whole earth is mine, 6 you will be for me a
kingdom of priests and a holy nation.' These are
the words you are to speak to the Israelites."

Exodus 19:3–6, NASB

you also, as living stones, are being built up as a spiritual house for **a holy priesthood, to offer up spiritual sacrifices** acceptable to God through Jesus Christ.

1 Peter 2:5

But you are a chosen race, a royal priesthood, a Holy Nation, A people for God's own possession, **so that you may proclaim the excellencies of Him who has called** you out of darkness into His marvelous light;

1 Peter 2:9

and He has made us to be a kingdom, priests to His God and Father--to Him be the glory and the dominion forever and ever. Amen.

Revelation 1:6

What happened after Jerusalem?

Did the lives of the followers of Jesus Christ reflect that they believed in the resurrection?

"You will be my witnesses in Jerusalem, Judea, Samaria and the ends of the earth."

Jesus

Acts is a historical book. When we understand the outline of the book of Acts it provides context for the rest of the New Testament letters.

It is important to our investigation to understand that Acts happens in real places, during real historical events, with real historical people. The events in Acts do not happen in isolation. Many of them are witnessed by thousands of people. Many of them are witnessed by entire cities. It is possible to go and to visit the exact places where the events occurred.

You can visit:

- Jerusalem,
- Caesarea,
- Athens,
- Corinth,
- Ephesus,
- Rome,

In fact, you can visit all of the places that are mentioned and actually stand in the spots where the events occurred.

You can stand on the steps in Jerusalem and see the places where 3,000 were baptized at Pentecost.

When you read in Acts 17 that Paul spoke to the people on Mars Hill, you do not need to imagine what that was like.

You can fly to Athens, Greece, and stand in the shadow of the Acropolis and look down on Socrates Temple in the Agora (marketplace).

When you read about Paul and his journey to Rome, you can visit Rome and see the Coliseum, and you can walk the streets and visit the area that would become the Jewish Ghetto.

You can also visit the ancient city of Corinth and stand in the marketplace where Paul would have sold his tents. You can stand on the Bema seat where his letters would have been read in public.

You can even walk to the end of the main road and place your hands and feet in the ancient starting blocks where the runner would have raced and inspired Paul to write,

Do you not know that in a race all the runners run, but only one gets the prize? Run in such a way as to get the prize.

1 Corinthians 9:24.

When you study and visit these places, it breathes life into the words of the Bible, and it is easier to recognize them as the testimony of eyewitnesses to the events that they write about.

In this part of our investigation, you will not only be examining the statements of the eyewitnesses, but you will be visiting the various places where the events occurred to help you gain historical context and understand the events in a new way.

Read like a Detective

The First Journey of Paul

Acts 13-14

The second half of the book of Acts records the missionary journeys of the Apostle Paul. It is estimated that Paul traveled over 10,000 miles during his visits to Greece, Italy, Turkey, Syria, and throughout Israel.

In his second letter to the church in Corinth, Paul described his journeys to his friends.

"Three times I was beaten with rods, once I was pelted with stones, three times I was shipwrecked, I spent a night and a day in the open sea, I have been constantly on the move. I have been in danger from rivers, in danger from bandits, in danger from my fellow Jews, in danger from Gentiles; in danger in the city, in danger in the country, in danger at sea; and in danger from false believers. I have labored and toiled and have often gone without sleep; I have known hunger and thirst and have often gone without food; I have been cold and naked."

2 Corinthians 11:25–27

Pauls' first missionary journey recorded in Acts 13-14 included John Mark, Barnabas, and Luke as part of his traveling team.

Some of his stops include:

- Antioch (Syria)
- Cyprus
- Galatia
- Iconium
- Lystra
- Derbe
- Iconium

It is important to note that while they were led and empowered by the Holy Spirit that Paul and his companions receive mixed receptions and mixed results.

Some receive the good news about the risen Messiah with joy while others harden their hearts and persecute the team. Often, they are forced to leave town for fear of their lives.

Once, in Lystra, the people drag Paul outside of the city, stone him and leave him for dead. Paul recovers, perhaps with the help of Dr. Luke, and eventually, Paul and Barnabas continue their mission and head to Derbe where the people receive the Good News, and many follow Jesus.

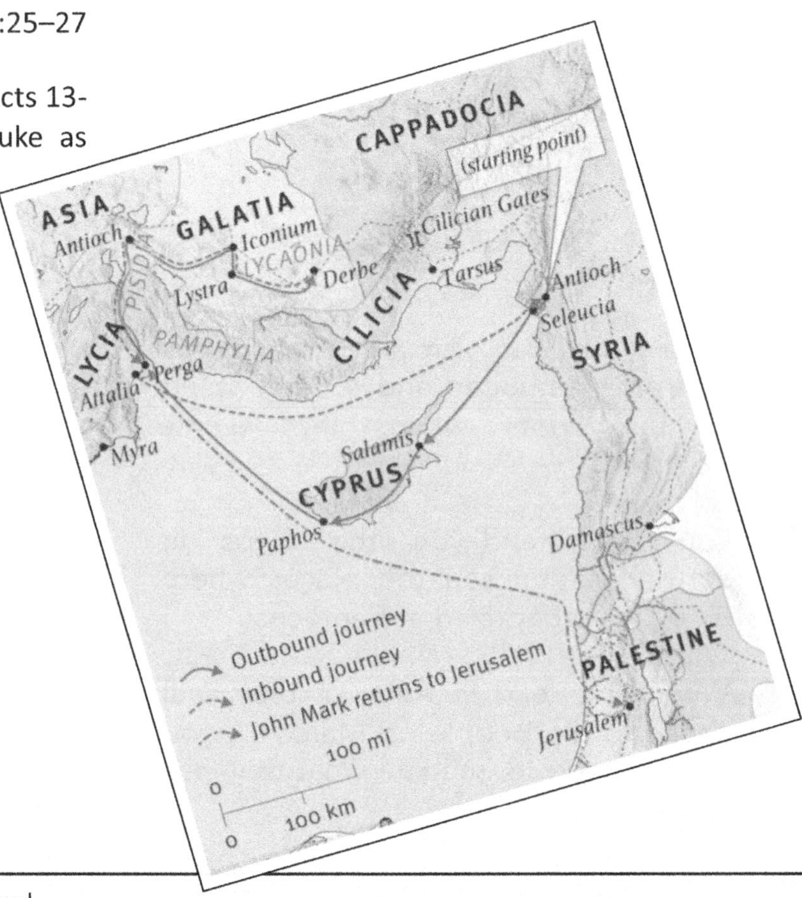

The Second Journey of Paul

Acts 15:36-18:22

At the beginning of the second missionary journey, there is a division between Paul and Barnabas.

Barnabas desired that John Mark accompany them on the journey, but Paul cites the fact that he had abandoned them in the past and refuses.

The result is two journeys that take place.

First, Barnabas and John Mark head to Cyrpus while Paul teams up with Silas and heads to Asia Minor.

Some of the stops on this journey include:

- Neapolis,
- Philippi,
- Thessalonica,
- Berea,
- Athens,
- Corinth,
- Ephesus,
- Caesarea

Joining Paul along the way is a young man named Timothy, who Paul begins to disciple and would later write two letters to the young man who would eventually plant a church in Ephesus.

Paul and his team begin to head north when he receives a vision from God telling him to go to Greece. The team boards a boat and sails to Philippi, where Lydia becomes a follower of Christ and invites the team to stay in her home.

Paul and Silas cast an evil spirit out of a young woman but end up being arrested in a heartbreaking turn of events when the man who had been profiting off of her condition accused them of ruining his business.

Rather than rejoicing in the young woman's new freedom, the authorities strip, beat, and throw Paul and Silas into prison.

That evening, God sends an earthquake that blows the doors off of the prison. This causes the jailer to panic. Thinking that he would be held responsible for a prison escape, he prepares to end his life.

But in an amazing demonstration of faith and commitment to the mission of God, Paul and Silas inform the jailer that in spite of the opportunity to escape that all of the prisoners are present and accounted for.

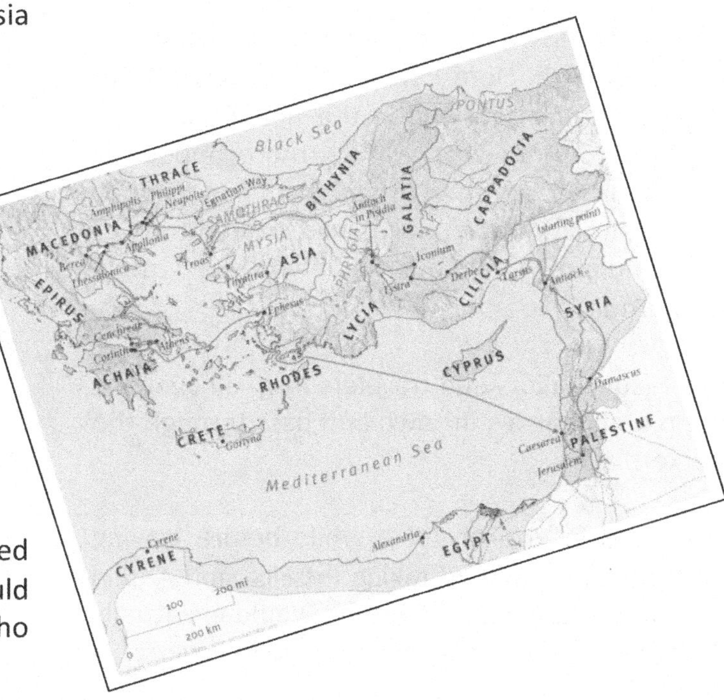

As a result, the jailer hears the Gospel, and he and his entire household are baptized.

The next morning the authorities release Paul and Silas, but Paul informs them that both he and Silas are citizens of Rome, and as such both, their beating and their imprisonment were against the law. In response, the local officials beg them to leave the area.

From there, the team stays in northern Greece and travels to Thessaloniki, where they are able to stay for a few weeks teaching in the synagogue before they are chased out of town.

Read like a Detective

Both Timothy and Silas stay in Berea, but Paul and Dr. Luke continue south to Athens. In Athens, he goes to the agora (marketplace) and begins to interact with the Greek Intellectuals near Socrates Temple and in the shadow of the Acropolis.

It is here that Paul delivers his famous sermon from Mars Hill overlooking the Agora area. Today you can stand on Mars Hill and still look down on Socrates Temple and visit the Acropolis.

Leaving Athens, Paul is joined by Timothy and Silas in Corinth. Here Paul joins Priscilla and her husband Aquila working in the marketplace. At the time, Corinth was a much more populated and important city than Athens. A major seaport, the Corinthian marketplace, was located next to the Temple of Apollo and in view of the Temple of Aphrodite.

As a result, sailors and travelers from all over the world would arrive in town and pass through the marketplace.

Paul stays in Corinth for a while before leaving Timothy and Silas and taking Priscilla and Aquila with him to Ephesus, where he would eventually leave the couple to disciple the new believers.

Paul then returned home to Jerusalem via the port city of Caesarea.

Some of the stops on the third journey include:

- Antioch
- Galatia
- Ephesus
- Corinth
- Philippi
- Asia (multiple)
- Rhodes
- Syria
- Caesarea
- Jerusalem

The Third Journey of Paul

Acts 18:23-21:14

Starting in Antioch, Paul returns to Galatia in Asia Minor before returning to Ephesus, where he stays for two years.

After beginning in the synagogue, the ministry in Ephesus expands to a local theatre. After more people begin turning to Christ for salvation, a man who made a living selling idols attempts to turn the people against Paul, but the local officials come to Paul's defense, and the ministry continues.

After two years, Paul returns to Greece, where he learns of a threat to his life. Leaving Greece he travels to Troas and then travels by ship, eventually returning to the port city of Caesarea.

During this time, Paul is warned not to return to Jerusalem. Knowing that he will be arrested if he returns, his team and friends beg him not to go.

But Paul, feeling led by God, returns and is arrested. Eventually, he stands trial before Governor Festus and King Agrippa.

The Prison Years

Arriving in Jerusalem, Paul is arrested and falsely charged with defiling the temple. A riot starts, and Paul is rescued by the Roman soldiers who were policing the area.

The following day, Paul appears before the Sanhedrin. A former Pharisee himself, Paul realizes that there are both Pharisees and Sadducees represented in the Sanhedrin, and he crafts his defense around his belief in that Jesus is the resurrected Messiah.

Soon Paul is forgotten, and the Pharisees and Sadducees begin arguing among themselves. The Pharisees, who believe in the resurrection of the dead side with Paul while the Sadducees who do not argue against him.

Later in the evening, Paul receives of vision of Christ informing him that he will end up in Rome.

Learning of a new plot to kill Paul, the Romans escort Paul out of Jerusalem to the protection of the Roman Governor Felix, who was stationed in Caesarea.

After a quick trial, Felix discerns that there is nothing to the charges against Paul but not wanting to cause a problem with the Jewish leadership he keeps Paul under a loose form of house arrest for two years.

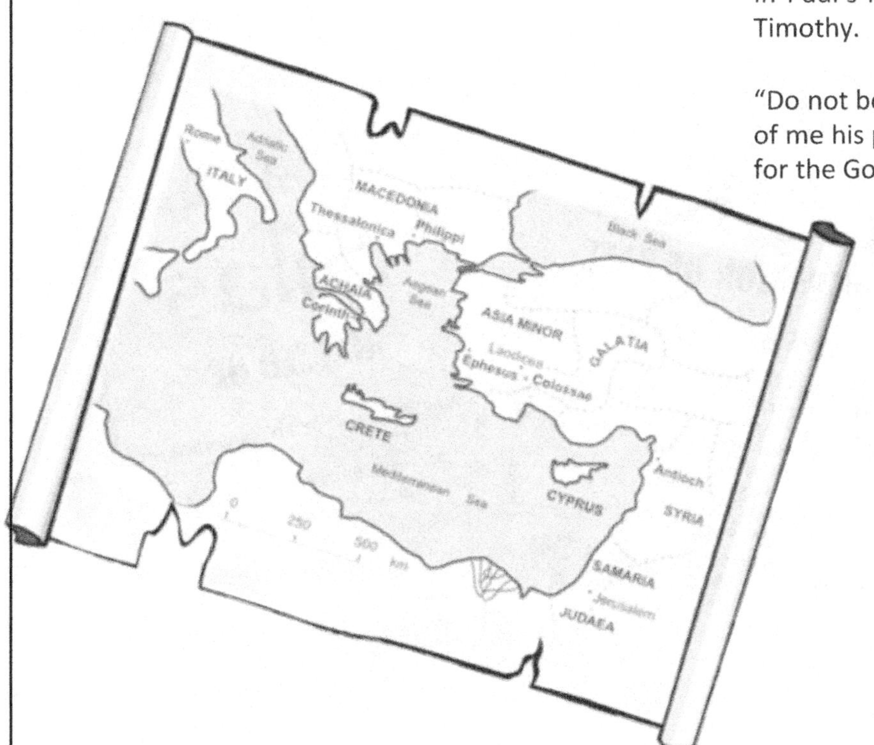

When Festus replaced Felix, he wastes little time before stating his desire to move Paul back to Jerusalem for trial. But knowing that would result in certain unjustified death he appeals to his right as a Roman citizen to appear before Caesar.

But Festus finds himself caught in a tough situation. The law stated that he must honor Paul's request and send him to Rome for trial, but he is unsure what to charge him with. A few days, later the great-grandson of Herod the Great, King Herod Agrippa II visited Caesarea with his sister Bernice. Together the three of them invite Paul to present his defense before them.

It was during his defense that King Agrippa stated, "you almost persuade me to become a Christian" (Acts 26:28).

It was during his imprisonment that Paul wrote several letters before sailing to Rome, where he lived under house arrest while awaiting his trial before Caesar.

Today you can visit Caesarea and see the home along the coast where it is believed that Paul stayed during his time in Caesarea. Within walking distance, you can see the Governor's palace, an Amphitheatre, and a hippodrome.

In Paul's last known letter, he writes these words to Timothy.

"Do not be ashamed of the testimony of our Lord, nor of me his prisoner, but share with me in the sufferings for the Gospel according to the power of God."

2 Timothy 1:8

Think like a Detective

What does the evidence say?

Parts of the book of Acts read like a prison novel. The same men who had abandoned their rabbi went to prison and lost their lives after boldly proclaiming their belief that Jesus of Nazareth was the Messiah who died for the sins of the world and rose from the dead to conquer the grave.

The evidence board

Is Paul's claim correct? Is Jesus the promised Messiah?

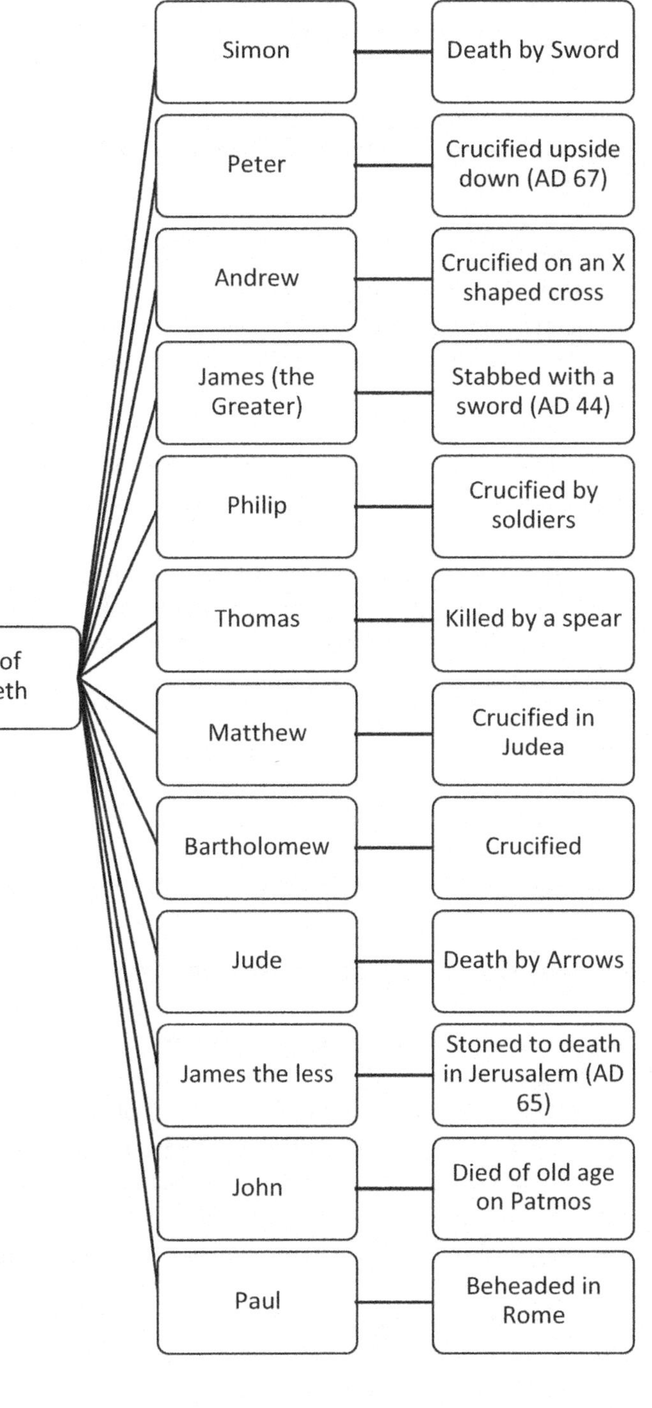

It was not just a few people who were impacted because of their unwavering belief in the resurrection of Jesus as the Messiah.

The non-Christian Roman historian Suetonius (69-140AD) wrote about the way Emperor Claudius (41-54AD) treated the Christians. His report is important on several levels. First, as a non-Christian, he is presenting an unbiased view of the events the way he understood them. Second, the reign of Claudius would have still been in the lifetime of Peter, Paul, and the other apostles time in Rome.

Here is what he wrote:

"Because the Jews at Rome caused constant disturbances at the instigation of (Christ), (Claudius) expelled them from the city of Rome.

(Life of Claudius, 25:4).

This expulsion took place in 49AD, just a few short years after Christ would have risen from the dead. So the impact of eyewitnesses who would have been in Jerusalem for the feast of Passover and for the feast of Pentecost would have still been in full effect to verify the validity of the events.

Suetonius also wrote about the fire that destroyed Rome at the hands of Nero. Nero burned the city of Rome and then blamed the Christians for the fire. A series of punishments and persecution followed.

The evidence board

Is Paul's claim correct? Is Jesus the promised Messiah?

The Ancient Global Mission of God Project

For this project, you will have the opportunity to explore an area of learning that you are personally interested in.

The book of Acts traces the story of the Golden Thread of God that started in Eden with the mandate to fill the earth with God's glory as it played out in the years following the life of Jesus Christ.

That thread ran through the middle east, Asia, Africa, Greece, Italy, and many other places.

It is sometimes easy to displace the Bible and to view it as something that did not happen in real-time and in the context of other historical places and events.

Your mission for this investigation is to pick someone, someplace or something from that time period, research it, build a model that will help your fellow investigation team to understand what you learned, and then to present your findings.

In many ways, your options are limitless.

You can choose to study the Ancient marketplace in Athens, the Acropolis, Mars Hill, the impact of Greek or Roman gods on the spread of the gospel, The Roman Coliseum, The Roman Fire, The Roman Circus Maximus, The Palace in Caesarea where Paul was held Prisoner, Ephesus, Ancient Sailing Vessels which would have provided transportation during the missionary journeys, or you can study the life of one of the twelve disciples of Jesus Christ and learn what is known about their faith, their testimony, and their death.

Your assignment is to research, investigate, and then create something that will help visually illustrate what you have learned.

Evidence board ideas

Exploring the known world at the time of the early church.

The Roman Pantheon

Located in Rome, it is a temple to "honor all gods." The purpose of the Pantheon was to honor and worship all gods.
The first version of the Pantheon is believed to have been built in 27BC, with the modern version being built in 120 AD by Emperor Hadrian.

One of the most famous parts of the structure is the hole in the middle of the top of the dome. Each year at exactly noon on April 21, the date that Romans believe the city was founded, the sunlight shines through the hole and strikes a metal object above the door that illuminates the area with light.

The Roman Colosseum

Over 60,000 Jewish slaves built the Colosseum in only nine years. It is an amazing feat since the building seats over 50,000 people but has 84 gates that would allow people to enter or exit in under 20 minutes.

Structurally it is a marvel. When it rained, the Romans could stretch a red canvas over the entire top. They also had the option to fill the floor with water to reenact sea battles.

The Colosseum opened in 80AD when Emperor Titus held the inaugural games.

Games could last up to 100 days at a time and came at an enormous cost of life.

400,000 people and over 1 million animals lost their lives in the Colosseum.

In 107AD, Emperor Trajan was responsible for the lives of 10,000 gladiators and 11,000 animals who died during a celebration that lasted for 123 days.

True Hero

The Sermon on Mars Hill

While Paul was waiting for them in Athens,
he was greatly distressed to see that the city
was full of idols. 17 So he reasoned in the
synagogue with both Jews and God-fearing
Greeks, as well as in the marketplace day by
day with those who happened to be
there. 18 A group of Epicurean and Stoic
philosophers began to debate with him.
Some of them asked, "What is this babbler
trying to say?" Others remarked, "He seems
to be advocating foreign gods." They said
this because Paul was preaching the good
news about Jesus and the
resurrection. 19 Then they took him and
brought him to a meeting of the
Areopagus, where they said to him, "May
we know what this new teaching is that you
are presenting? 20 You are bringing some
strange ideas to our ears, and we would like
to know what they mean."21 (All the
Athenians and the foreigners who lived
there spent their time doing nothing but
talking about and listening to the latest
ideas.)

22 Paul then stood up in the meeting of the
Areopagus and said: "People of Athens! I
see that in every way you are very
religious. 23 For as I walked around and
looked carefully at your objects of worship, I
even found an altar with this inscription: to
an unknown god. So you are ignorant of the
very thing you worship—and this is what I
am going to proclaim to you.

24 **"The God who made the world and
everything in it is the Lord of heaven and
earth and does not live in temples built by
human hands.** 25 **And he is not served by
human hands, as if he needed anything.
Rather, he himself gives everyone life and
breath and everything else.**

26 **From one man he made all the nations,
that they should inhabit the whole earth;
and he marked out their appointed times
in history and the boundaries of their
lands.**

27 **God did this so that they would seek
him and perhaps reach out for him and
find him, though he is not far from any
one of us.** 28 **'For in him we live and move
and have our being.' As some of your own
poets have said, 'We are his offspring.'**

29 "Therefore since we are God's offspring,
we should not think that the divine being is
like gold or silver or stone—an image made
by human design and skill.

30 In the past God overlooked such
ignorance, but now he commands all people
everywhere to repent. 31 For he has set a
day when he will judge the world with
justice by the man he has appointed. He has
given proof of this to everyone by raising
him from the dead."

The Apostle Paul
Acts 17

TRUE HERO

"The true story of the extraordinary mission of God"

TRUE HERO

"The true story of the extraordinary mission of God"

promised

Learning to love God's Word

So God created mankind in His own *image*, in the *image* of God He created them; male and female He created them. God blessed them and said to them,

"Be fruitful and increase in number; fill the earth and subdue it."

Genesis 1:27-28

The Future Kingdom of God

1 2 3 4 5 6 7

ACT II BEGINS BY INFORMING US THAT GOD IS COMMITTED TO FULFILLING HIS MISSION, AND ENDS WITH ETERNAL SHALOM

In Act I, scene 5 of the Hebrew Scriptures, God appoints Joshua (Yeshua, God's deliverer) to lead His people into the land flowing with milk and honey. The land that He promised to them.

They anoint a king, build a temple where heaven and earth meet, and commit to reflecting the glory of God to the nations of the world.

In Act 2, scene 5, Yeshua (Jesus of Nazareth) returns to Jerusalem. He walks into the Temple and sets up His kingdom on earth.

It is the rising tension that leads to the culmination of the plot of God's story.

But unlike the parts of the Bible that are historical (the parts that have already happened in the past) scenes, 5,6, and 7 will occur at some point in the future.

And unlike the parts where a close examination of the evidence leads to a consensus and understanding of exactly what has happened in the past, there are people who genuinely love Jesus who hold different understandings as to what Jesus has promised will happen in the future.

Many books have been written attempting to examine and clearly explain to the best of human understanding what God has promised will happen in the future.

There are a number of things that people do not agree on, but there area a few things God has specifically revealed.

The Coming Kingdom of God

The first time that the Messiah walked the earth, it was prophesied that he would ride into Jerusalem on the back of a donkey.

Rejoice greatly, Daughter Zion!
Shout, Daughter Jerusalem!
See, your king comes to you,
righteous and victorious,
lowly and riding on a donkey,
on a colt, the foal of a donkey.

Zechariah 9:9

Jesus sent two disciples, [2] saying to them, "Go to the village ahead of you, and at once you will find a donkey tied there, with her colt by her. Untie them and bring them to me.[3] If anyone says anything to you, say that the Lord needs them, and he will send them right away."
[4] This took place to fulfill what was spoken through the prophet:

[5] "Say to Daughter Zion, 'See, your king comes to you, gentle and riding on a donkey,
and on a colt, the foal of a donkey.'"

[6] The disciples went and did as Jesus had instructed them. [7] They brought the donkey and the colt and placed their cloaks on them for Jesus to sit on. [8] A very large crowd spread their cloaks on the road, while others cut branches from the trees and spread them on the road. [9] The crowds that went ahead of him and those that followed shouted,

Matthew 21:1-12

The second time that the Messiah will come, he will not be arriving as the humble priest but as the conquering King of kings and Lord of Lords.

He will not be riding a humble donkey but on a white horse. He will not be conquering sin but will be setting up His kingdom.

11 I saw heaven standing open and there before me was a white horse, whose rider is called Faithful and True. With justice he judges and wages war. 12 His eyes are like blazing fire, and on his head are many crowns. He has a name written on him that no one knows but he himself. 13 He is dressed in a robe dipped in blood, and his name is the Word of God. 14 The armies of heaven were following him, riding on white horses and dressed in fine linen, white and clean. 15 Coming out of his mouth is a sharp sword with which to strike down the nations. "He will rule them with an iron scepter."[a] He treads the winepress of the fury of the wrath of God Almighty. 16 On his robe and on his thigh he has this name written: king of kings and lord of lords.

Revelation 19:11-16

The Coming Kingdom of God

The Purple Thread

Plot. How does the story end?

REVELATION 7:7-12

After this I looked, and there before me was a great multitude that no one could count, from every nation, tribe, people and language, standing before the throne and before the Lamb. They were wearing white robes and were holding palm branches in their hands. [10] And they cried out in a loud voice:

"Salvation belongs to our God, who sits on the throne, and to the Lamb."[11] All the angels were standing around the throne and around the elders and the four living creatures. They fell down on their faces before the throne and worshiped God, [12] saying: "Amen! Praise and glory and wisdom and thanks and honorand power and strength be to our God for ever and ever. Amen!"

REVELATION 7:7-12

REVELATION 21: 1-6,10

A NEW HEAVEN AND A NEW EARTH

21 Then I saw "a new heaven and a new earth," for the first heaven and the first earth had passed away, and there was no longer any sea. [2] I saw the Holy City, the new Jerusalem, coming down out of heaven from God, prepared as a bride beautifully dressed for her husband. [3] And I heard a loud voice from the throne saying, "Look! God's dwelling place is now among the people, and he will dwell with them. They will be his people, and God himself will be with them and be their God. [4] 'He will wipe every tear from their eyes. There will be no more death' or mourning or crying or pain, for the old order of things has passed away."

[5] He who was seated on the throne said, "I am making everything new!" Then he said, "Write this down, for these words are trustworthy and true."

[6] He said to me: "It is done. I am the Alpha and the Omega, the Beginning and the End... "Come, I will show you the bride, the wife of the Lamb."

[10] And he carried me away in the Spirit to a mountain great and high, and showed me the Holy City, Jerusalem, coming down out of heaven from God.

REVELATION 21:11-14, 22-27

[11] It shone with the glory of God, and its brilliance was like that of a very precious jewel, like a jasper, clear as crystal. [12] It had a great, high wall with twelve gates, and with twelve angels at the gates. On the gates were written the names of the twelve tribes of Israel. [13] There were three gates on the east, three on the north, three on the south and three on the west. [14] The wall of the city had twelve foundations, and on them were the names of the twelve apostles of the Lamb...

The great street of the city was of gold, as pure as transparent glass.

[22] I did not see a temple in the city, because the Lord God Almighty and the Lamb are its temple. [23] The city does not need the sun or the moon to shine on it, for the glory of God gives it light, and the Lamb is its lamp. [24] The nations will walk by its light, and the kings of the earth will bring their splendor into it. [25] On no day will its gates ever be shut, for there will be no night there. [26] The glory and honor of the nations will be brought into it. [27] Nothing impure will ever enter it, nor will anyone who does what is shameful or deceitful, but only those whose names are written in the Lamb's book of life.

The evidence board

Is Paul's claim correct? Is Jesus the promised Messiah?

For the Son of Man is going to come in his Father's glory with his angels, and then he will reward each person according to what they have done.

Matthew 16:27

"When the Son of Man comes in his glory, and all the angels with him, he will sit on his glorious throne.

Matthew 25:31

If anyone is ashamed of me and my words in this adulterous and sinful generation, the Son of Man will be ashamed of them when he comes in his Father's glory with the holy angels."

Mark 8:38

"At that time people will see the Son of Man coming in clouds with great power and glory.

Mark 13:26

Notes:

22 I did not see a temple in the city, because the Lord
God Almighty and the Lamb are its temple. 23 The city
does not need the sun or the moon to shine on it, for
the glory of God gives it light, and the Lamb is its
lamp. 24 The nations will walk by its light, and the kings
of the earth will bring their splendor into it. 25 On no
day will its gates ever be shut, for there will be no night
there. 26 The glory and honor of the nations will be
brought into it. 27 Nothing impure will ever enter it, nor
will anyone who does what is shameful or deceitful, but
only those whose names are written in the Lamb's book
of life.

Revelation 21:22-27

The evidence board

Is Paul's claim correct? Is Jesus the promised Messiah?

So God created man in his own image,
in the image of God he created him;
male and female he created them.
28 And God blessed them. And God said to
them, "Be fruitful and multiply and fill the
earth and subdue it,

Genesis 1:27-28

Now the Lord said to Abram, "Go from
your country and your kindred and your
father's house to the land that I will show
you. [2] And I will make of you a great nation,
and I will bless you and make your name
great, so that you will be a blessing. [3] I will
bless those who bless you, and him who
dishonors you I will curse, and in you all
the families of the earth shall be blessed."

Genesis 12:1-3

"All authority in heaven and on
earth has been given to me. [19] Go
therefore and make disciples of all
nations, baptizing them in the name
of the Father and of the Son and
of the Holy Spirit,

Matthew 28:18b-19

The God who made the world and everything in it,
being Lord of heaven and earth, does not live in
temples made by man, [25] nor is he served by human
hands, as though he needed anything, since he
himself gives to all mankind life and breath and
everything. [26] And he made from one man every nation
of mankind to live on all the face of the earth, having
determined allotted periods and the boundaries of
their dwelling place, [27] that they should seek God, and
perhaps feel their way toward him and find him. Yet he
is actually not far from each one of us,

Acts 17:24-27

[9] After this I looked, and behold, a
great multitude that no one could
number, from every nation, from
all tribes and peoples and
languages, standing before the
throne and before the
Lamb, clothed in white robes,
with palm branches in their
hands, [10] and crying out with a
loud voice, "Salvation belongs to
our God who sits on the throne,
and to the Lamb!"

[11] And all the angels were standing
around the throne and around the
elders and the four living
creatures, and they fell on their
faces before the throne and
worshiped God, [12] saying, "Amen!

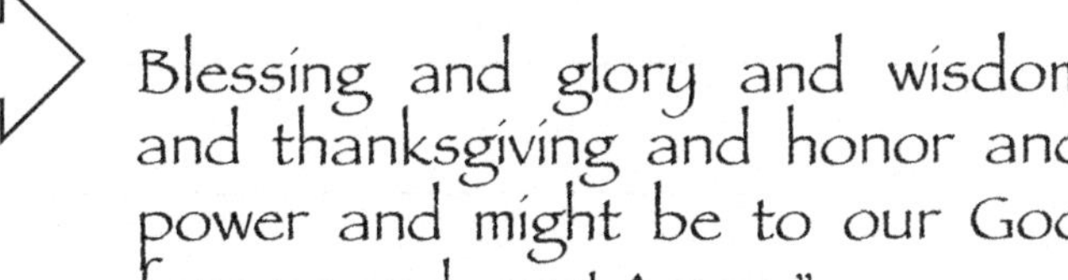

Blessing and glory and wisdom
and thanksgiving and honor and
power and might be to our God
forever and ever! Amen."

Revelation 7:9-12

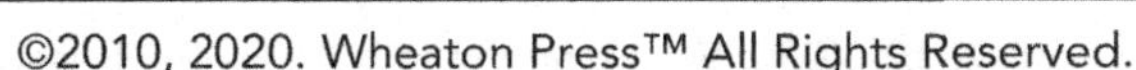

Investigation Summary

To be Submitted by Authorized Agents Only
Do not submit this document if it is wet or damp.

EVIDENCE

Source of Evidence: ______________________________

Summary Description of Evidence:

TRUE HERO

"The true story of the extraordinary mission of God"

proximity

Learning to love God's Word

After this I looked, and there before me was a great multitude that no one could count, from every nation, tribe, people and language, standing before the throne and before the Lamb...All the angels were standing around the throne... They fell down on their faces before the throne and worshiped God,

Revelation 7:9-11

Preparing for the trial

At the beginning of this investigation, you were chosen because of your understanding and expertise in the Hebrew Scriptures.

As you probably recall, it was during scene 6 that the people of God physically and spiritually moved away from the presence of God.

The results were catastrophic and led to the Assyrian and Babylonian exile.

In scene 6 of Act 2, the people of God enjoy the presence of God as God reintegrates reality in the new heaven and the new earth.

In this final unit, the question is personal. Now that you have seen the entire plot of Scripture and you have examined the evidence, what do you believe the evidence supports?

- Is Paul a reliable witness?
- Did Jesus of Nazareth fulfill the requirements for the promised Messiah?
- Did He claim to be God?
- Did He rise from the dead?
- Did the lives of those who followed Him support the idea that they believed in His resurrection and His claims?
- How will you respond?

The Trial manuscript of Paul before Agrippa

Acts 26

So Agrippa said to Paul, "You have permission to speak for yourself." Then Paul stretched out his hand and made his defense:
[2] "I consider myself fortunate that it is before you, King Agrippa, I am going to make my defense today against all the accusations of the Jews, [3] especially because you are familiar with all the customs and controversies of the Jews. Therefore I beg you to listen to me patiently.

[4] "My manner of life from my youth, spent from the beginning among my own nation and in Jerusalem, is known by all the Jews. [5] They have known for a long time, if they are willing to testify, that according to the strictest party of our religion I have lived as a Pharisee.

[6] And now I stand here on trial because of my hope in the promise made by God to our fathers, [7] to which our twelve tribes hope to attain, as they earnestly worship night and day. And for this hope I am accused by Jews, O king!

[8] Why is it thought incredible by any of you that God raises the dead?

[9] "I myself was convinced that I ought to do many things in opposing the name of Jesus of Nazareth.
[10] And I did so in Jerusalem. I not only locked up many of the saints in prison after receiving authority from the chief priests, but when they were put to death, I cast my vote against them. [11] And I punished them often in all the synagogues and tried to make them blaspheme, and in raging fury against them I persecuted them even to foreign cities.

[12] "In this connection I journeyed to Damascus with the authority and commission of the chief priests. [13] At midday, O king, I saw on the way a light from heaven, brighter than the sun, that shone around me and those who journeyed with me. [14] And when we had all fallen to the ground, I heard a voice saying to me in the Hebrew language, 'Saul, Saul, why are you persecuting me? It is hard for you to kick against the goads.' [15] And I said, 'Who are you, Lord?' And the Lord said, 'I am Jesus whom you are persecuting. ."

The Trial manuscript of Paul before Agrippa

Acts 26

[16] But rise and stand upon your feet, for I have appeared to you for this purpose, to appoint you as a servant and witness to the things in which you have seen me and to those in which I will appear to you,[17] delivering you from your people and from the Gentiles—to whom I am sending you [18] to open their eyes, so that they may turn from darkness to light and from the power of Satan to God, that they may receive forgiveness of sins and a place among those who are sanctified by faith in me.'

[19] "Therefore, O King Agrippa, I was not disobedient to the heavenly vision, [20] but declared first to those in Damascus, then in Jerusalem and throughout all the region of Judea, and also to the Gentiles, that they should repent and turn to God, performing deeds in keeping with their repentance.

[21] For this reason the Jews seized me in the temple and tried to kill me.[22] To this day I have had the help that comes from God, and so I stand here testifying both to small and great, saying nothing but what the prophets and Moses said would come to pass:[23] that the Christ must suffer and that, by being the first to rise from the dead, he would proclaim light both to our people and to the Gentiles."

[24] And as he was saying these things in his defense, Festus said with a loud voice, "Paul, you are out of your mind; your great learning is driving you out of your mind."

[25] But Paul said, "I am not out of my mind, most excellent Festus, but I am speaking true and rational words.[26] For the king knows about these things, and to him I speak boldly. For I am persuaded that none of these things has escaped his notice, for this has not been done in a corner. [27] King Agrippa, do you believe the prophets? I know that you believe." [28] And Agrippa said to Paul, "In a short time would you persuade me to be a Christian?" [29] And Paul said, "Whether short or long, I would to God that not only you but also all who hear me this day might become such as I am—except for these chains."
[30] Then the king rose, and the governor and Bernice and those who were sitting with them.[31] And when they had withdrawn, they said to one another, "This man is doing nothing to deserve death or imprisonment." [32] And Agrippa said to Festus, "This man could have been set free if he had not appealed to Caesar."

Investigation Summary

Thinking like a Jury.

Answering the Essential Questions

Belonging: Where do I fit?	Identity: Who am I?	Purpose: What will I do?

Beliefs

Values

Habits

Actions

How will I respond?

Made in the USA
Monee, IL
22 June 2024

60331813R00090